MW01264262

Presence of Mind

A practical introduction to mindfulness and meditation

Michael Mrazek, Ph.D.

with Alissa Mrazek, Ph.D.

and Kaita Mrazek

ISBN-13: 9-78-0999326701

To Ruby

CONTENTS

Preface   1

PART I: Attention

1   Standing Guard   4

2   What is Mindfulness?   7

3   Anchoring Attention   11

4   Mindfulness vs. Meditation   14

5   The Spotlight & Peripheral Awareness   18

6   The Misconception of the Quiet Mind   24

PART II: Thoughts, Evaluations, & Emotions

7   The Nature of Thoughts   28

8   Harnessing the Thinking Mind   32

9   Evaluation & the Conditions for Our Happiness   35

10   The Violence of Comparison   39

11   Self-Criticism & Judgment Loops   45

12   Releasing Unskillful Evaluations   49

13   Understanding Emotions   53

14   Willingness   56

15   Working with Difficult Emotions   61

16   Cultivating Positive Emotions   67

PART III: Meditation

17   Meditation   72

18   Present Moment Awareness Meditation   77

19   Mindful Breathing Meditation   82

20   Open Monitoring Meditation   86

21   Introspection   91

22   Effort   96

PART IV: The Obstacles

23   The Inevitable Obstacles   102

24   Drowsiness   107

25   Discomfort   112

26   Doubt   117

27   Ill-will   123

28   Restlessness   127

29   An Interlude on Happiness   131

30   Sensory Desire   137

PART V: Mastery

31   Establishing the Habit of Meditation   144

32   Mastery of Mindfulness   148

      Afterword   155

ACKNOWLEDGMENTS

Thank you Jonathan Schooler for nearly a decade of mentorship, without which this book would likely not exist. Thanks also to Jonathan Cloughesy, Abbey Holman, Alex Landry, Zoë Rathbun, Mark Estefanos, Theo Masters-Waage, and Leandro Calcagnotto for exploring these ideas so deeply and finding countless ways to improve this book.

i

PREFACE

I first dabbled in mindfulness during high school, but I became obsessed with it as I was starting graduate school in cognitive neuroscience. Naively thinking that there must be one best way to practice mindfulness, I spent years working through countless books and retreats to find it. Over time, I became more convinced of the value of mindfulness but also increasingly doubtful that I would find one superior approach. Every teacher I encountered had their preferred set of strategies, and one wise teacher's instructions would sometimes even contradict another's. All the different perspectives made it hard to know which approach was best.

I'm now convinced there is no single best way. There are lots of ways to understand and practice mindfulness, and many of them lead to good results. This book presents an approach that has emerged from my obsessive practice, study, research, and teaching of mindfulness over the last decade. Our research at the University of California Santa Barbara has repeatedly shown that this approach is highly effective at helping people use mindfulness to improve their lives in a myriad of ways. Yet still, that doesn't mean it is the one and only right path. My hope is that it will offer you a clear, practical, science-based, secular, and occasionally humorous introduction to something that has forever improved my life. If this approach to mindfulness inspires you, make sure to study others that will offer you complementary perspectives.

When reading a book about mindfulness, there is a risk that it will become just another thing we know we should do rather than a tool we regularly use to improve the quality of our lives. There is a world of difference between knowing what to do and doing what we know. Developing a detailed understanding of mindfulness is helpful, but there is even greater value in applying that understanding to our lives. To study mindfulness without practicing it would be like going to a highly rated restaurant only to meticulously study the menu without actually ordering anything. The menu itself is valuable, but mostly in pointing you to something of still greater value. To fully benefit from mindfulness, you will need to test it out in the laboratory of your life. This book will provide you with perspective and strategies that will help you do that successfully.

Part I:

ATTENTION

1 – STANDING GUARD

The scientific literature shows that mindfulness can improve an incredible number of things that truly matter in our lives. Research indicates that mindfulness can improve our physical health, reduce our stress, strengthen our relationships, help us think more clearly, and make us happier—not to mention that it can help treat a wide range of mental illnesses. I don't know about you, but when I read a list like that it sets off warning bells in my mind. How could mindfulness be so good for so many different things?

After reading hundreds of scientific papers, conducting numerous experiments on the effects of mindfulness training, and exploring the impact of mindfulness in my own life, I found that my skepticism wore off. I've come to understand that the far reaching relevance of mindfulness is real. It stems from the way mindfulness influences our *attention*. When most people think about attention, they think about how long they can focus. That's an important aspect, but there's much more to it.

In any moment, there are countless things occurring in our environment, body, and mind. Without us realizing it, our attention sifts through everything that's happening and filters most of it out. We become consciously aware of only a tiny fraction of the things we *could* experience. When attention works effectively, we become aware of the things that deserve further consideration while everything else slips past unnoticed. As you read this chapter, your attention is working continuously to ensure that the words on this page aren't drowned out by the hundreds of other things happening within and around you. (You're doing well, keep it up!)

This filtering of experience is true not only of what we see and hear, but also of what we think. Thousands of thoughts flicker through our heads every day, and attention controls which of these we elaborate. Because attention influences both what we perceive and what we think, it also influences what emotions we feel. This means that where we focus our attention is one of the most powerful influences over what we experience. Yet many people never recognize that they can take control over this process, and even fewer learn how to do it well. You can dramatically improve your ability to use attention effectively, and that can profoundly shape your entire life. Mindfulness lets you stand guard at the door of your mind and have greater choice over how you relate to everything you experience.

Attention is a natural ability that allows each of us to navigate our environments and our lives. It accomplishes small wonders each time you drive, hold a conversation, or even just read this book. Yet almost no one uses attention optimally. Can you focus on what you like, when you like, for as long you like? In an era of sound bites and social media, many people now struggle to focus for more than just a few minutes. And more importantly, how might your life be different if you could use your attention to more skillfully guide your thoughts, emotions, and actions on a moment-by-moment basis? Mindfulness uses attention to influence what we experience and how we relate to those experiences, so it has the potential to improve almost everything.

2 – WHAT IS MINDFULNESS?

The word *mindfulness* is used with a growing sense of familiarity in scientific research and popular culture, but what exactly does it mean? When you try to pin down precisely what scientists, clinicians, teachers, and contemplatives mean when they use the word *mindfulness*, you find that there is no universally accepted definition. To the contrary, there are many perspectives—and even disagreement—regarding what the word mindfulness should convey.

The one quality of mindfulness that most everyone can agree on is being truly present with whatever you're doing. This presence of mind allows us to be completely dialed in at an important meeting or to catch every word as our partner recounts their day. We all know how good it feels to be with someone who is fully present to us, and yet we often struggle to be present ourselves. In fact, the empirical literature suggests we spend about a third to a half of our waking life engaging with one thing while thinking about something else.

The second most commonly emphasized quality of mindfulness is letting go of the compulsion to immediately evaluate everything that happens to us. Without even realizing it, we make evaluations in almost every waking moment. We judge our thoughts, our emotions, other people, the weather, and perhaps most of all we judge ourselves. Many of these evaluations are both unnecessary and unhelpful, and mindfulness involves letting go of counterproductive evaluations. Yet as we will discuss in detail, this does not imply that you should abandon critical thinking and discernment. To the contrary, discernment must help guide our choice of which evaluations to let go and which to endorse.

I like to express these two primary qualities of mindfulness as *non-judgmental presence of mind*. Although this is consistent with most contemporary uses of the word mindfulness, some suggest that mindfulness also involves other qualities like openness, curiosity, acceptance, or even the tendency to describe or label our experiences. This proliferation of definitions is a natural result of many people exploring overlapping strategies for cultivating the mind and finding unique forms of expression and emphasis. Although this might lead mindfulness to appear convoluted, I believe there is a beautiful elegance and clarity beneath the disagreement. You just have to ask a different question. Rather than focus on definitions, focus on actual mechanics. What specifically must you do to apply mindfulness in your life?

There are two fundamental skills to mindfulness. In any moment, we must be able to *attend* and *release*. Although these are exceedingly valuable skills, they are widely unappreciated and rarely trained. *Attending* is simply focusing your attention—something most people readily understand. We do this all the time. We attend to countless things every day by sustaining attention even briefly on some specific aspect of our experience. You're doing it right now by focusing on the words in this chapter. Yet if you try to attend to just one thing for long, you will quickly notice that distractions inevitably arise. To stay fully present with any one thing, we must be able to *release* all the distractions. Releasing interrupts an otherwise habitual tendency to elaborate on our thoughts and experiences. For example, we have a strong tendency to engage with all the thoughts that pop into our minds by elaborating them into extended narratives rather than letting them simply pass by. We can choose to release those thoughts instead. By not engaging with them, we allow them to fade away naturally. It's not pushing away, but letting go.

The way we use our hands is a good metaphor for attending and releasing. We need to be able to reach and grab things, but we also need to be able to put them down. Without both the ability to grab and to release, our hands wouldn't function. Attention works the same way.

Attending and releasing are deeply intertwined, but we will explore ways they can be used separately in later chapters. They are centrally relevant to every form of mindfulness and meditation, and they can be cultivated to exceptional levels. Cultivating these skills over time allows us to be more present with the things that truly matter in life. This is far from trivial. Research from our laboratory has shown that this presence of mind can lead to better performance on challenging measures of cognitive abilities—including high-stakes standardized tests like the GRE. Research also shows that mindfulness can reduce stress and negative emotions, in part by changing the way we relate to the thoughts running through our heads. And as we learn to cultivate these skills, research shows that mindfulness eventually makes people *happier*. These benefits—and many others—ultimately derive from the skills of attending and releasing. The use of these two simple skills holds the power to change our entire lives. This is the beautiful simplicity of mindfulness. Yet to truly appreciate the richness of mindfulness—and to understand how to best cultivate and apply it in our lives—there is much more to discuss.

3 – ANCHORING ATTENTION

You can be mindful of anything—touch, sights, sounds, smells, tastes, emotions, or thoughts. Our lives are filled with an endless array of these experiences, and usually our attention darts frantically between them. But if we wish, we can learn to *anchor* our awareness on a subset of our experiences so that we are not swept away by distractions.

If we can be mindful of anything, what does that mean in practice? Using an anchor means choosing a specific target or focus for our attention and deciding to bring ourselves back every time we get distracted. The target of our mindfulness can be either broad or narrow. It can be as broad as everything occurring in the present moment or as narrow as the physical sensations of breathing. Throughout the day, the target of our mindfulness shifts frequently so that we can skillfully allocate our attention as needed. We can be mindful as we write an email by giving it our full attention and then seamlessly switch our anchor to a conversation as we take a phone call. Our anchor changes thousands of times a day, and being more deliberate about this process allows us to be fully present with whatever we're currently doing.

When we are mindful of the present—something we will call *present moment awareness*—we release any thoughts about the past or future. We can direct our attention to anything that is occurring right now. It may be our five senses, our emotional state, or even thoughts related to the immediate present. Within this wide range of experiences, we are still mindful even as our attention jumps from one thing to the next. As long as we don't get swept away by thoughts of the past and future, we are mindfully anchored in the present.

Initially, it can seem counterintuitive that it is possible to be mindful even as our attention is alternating between multiple things. But consider how often in life doing *one* thing really means paying attention to several. To sit down and share a meal, your attention will have to fluctuate at least between your food and your companions. Even if you choose to eat a meal in silence by yourself, your attention will still alternate between the food you see on your plate and the way it tastes in your mouth. Even as your focus shifts back and forth, you can still remain grounded in present moment awareness.

If present moment awareness represents a broad target for our mindfulness, a classic example of a narrow focus is mindful breathing. When we are mindful of our breath, we let go of not only the past and future but also of any other experiences that compete for our attention. If we try to narrow our attention to only the sensations of breathing, we can be sure that distractions will arise. There may be discomfort in our bodies, sounds from the other room, or thoughts about the people surrounding us. All of these are in the immediate present, but to be mindful of our breath we must release them.

It's a useful exercise to explore what it means to be mindful during different kinds of experiences to make sure you understand how to apply the concept of the anchor. I remember having one student who proudly shared that she had been so mindful of the pretty landscape while driving that she had missed her exit. She probably chose the wrong anchor. Mindful driving is actually an informative example because it is narrower than present moment awareness but broader than mindful breathing. While driving, there are many different things requiring your attention. You need to constantly update your awareness of where you are relative to other cars on the road, but you also need to monitor for road signs and keep track of your speed. To drive mindfully, you anchor your attention on the set of things that are crucial to monitor and allow your attention to alternate between them. However, driving doesn't require an awareness of your breath or even an appreciation of the view. Sometimes people mistakenly try to practice mindfulness by staying aware of their breath even while changing lanes or merging into traffic. You might choose to direct your attention to the view or your breath temporarily, but these are ultimately distractions from driving.

The concept of an anchor is central to practicing mindfulness. It requires that you be clear about where you are choosing to focus your attention. To bring mindfulness into our daily lives, we must become more intentional about where we want to direct our minds. Deliberately making this choice even a little more often throughout our days is a huge initial step to increasing our presence of mind.

4 - MINDFULNESS VS. MEDITATION

One attractive feature of mindfulness is that we can practice without taking any time away from our busy lives. We can be mindful while eating, working, or making love. On the other hand, meditation involves setting time aside for dedicated practice of mindfulness. This can be a barrier for people starting the practice. Many people who are new to mindfulness view meditation as a subtraction of time from their lives that they could spend on other important things. My days are very full too, so I get it. But meditation is actually a great addition to our busy lives, and it multiples the rate at which our mindfulness can develop.

When we take some time each day to fully commit to cultivating our minds in formal meditation, our skill at attending and releasing improves quickly. By temporarily setting aside all other priorities, meditation creates an opportunity to cultivate mindfulness that is harder to come by in daily life. It's like an athlete refining a skill over and over during practice until they can use it effortlessly during a game. It's easier to practice attending and releasing during meditation when they can be the absolute priority. This dedicated practice then translates into being able to use these skills much more effectively in daily life.

There are many different kinds of meditation, each with a somewhat distinct purpose. Some forms of meditation help you develop focused attention, while others cultivate specific emotions like gratitude or compassion. In later chapters, we will discuss several different types of meditation and review detailed instructions for how to practice them. For now, we will briefly explore the relationship between mindfulness and one specific practice often called *focused attention meditation*. This is the most common method of meditation you are likely to encounter, and it is also an excellent place to begin.

Focused attention meditation is practiced by trying to keep your attention directed to a specific anchor. One of the most commonly used anchors for meditation is the breath. Each time that we notice that we have become distracted from the sensations of breathing, we gently return our attention back to the breath. Taking time out of your day to simply watch your breath strikes many people as a little bizarre, if not a complete waste of time. That's understandable because it's not intuitive that sitting quietly and paying attention to something as simple as the breath could meaningfully change our lives and even make us happy. Yet both the scientific literature and millions of individuals' experiences indicate that something powerful can unfold as we sit quietly observing our breath.

I can personally vouch for this, as some of the happiest moments in my life have occurred during and after meditation. I can vividly recall one of the first times I emerged from a focused meditation into a world where nothing particularly special was happening and yet everything seemed different. My awareness was exceptionally clear and I felt completely unburdened by any subtle insecurities or nagging worries. That lightness faded over time as old habits of mind returned, but my understanding of mindfulness and meditation underwent a lasting change. I had experienced a brief moment in which many of my biases and filters had dropped away—filters that so consistently shaped my experience that I hadn't even noticed their presence. This eye-opening experience only arose because I had consistently made time to cultivate mindfulness during meditation, and the outcome was a new appreciation and commitment to bring mindfulness into my daily life.

Regular meditation makes it much easier to be mindful throughout the rest of our day, and the reverse is also true: being mindful in daily life allows us to sink more deeply into meditation. This was memorably illustrated to me by Reb Anderson, a prominent meditation teacher. He explained that Samurai warriors—who sometimes found themselves in mortal combat—were devoted to practicing mindfulness in even the smallest daily activities. In combat, their lives depended on their ability to be fully present. Even a small lapse of attention could be fatal. To ensure they could be completely present during combat, they also practiced being completely present during every moment of their day. They brought mindfulness to the all little things, like pouring a cup of tea.

The stakes may not be as high when we sit to meditate, but the principle still applies. If you can't be fully present with your family, you probably won't be able to be fully present with your breath during meditation. This isn't to say that we have to be mindful every waking moment—or even that we should strive for that. But if you neglect mindfulness during most of your waking hours and then sit down to meditate with high expectations, you may be disappointed. It's similar to how you can't be an elite athlete for only twenty minutes out of the day.

Of course, not everyone strives to be an athlete—but striving to be healthy is also great. It's just important to recognize that the more you practice mindfulness during daily life, the more quickly your meditations will become satisfying and transformative experiences. The ideal scenario is that both a daily meditation practice and the habit of bringing mindfulness into everyday experiences reinforce one another in an upward cycle toward a happy life.

5 – THE SPOTLIGHT & PERIPHERAL AWARENESS

I may have misled you. Let me explain. In the first chapter, I introduced the idea that attention acts as a filter. That's true. I also described how our brains are constantly bombarded with more information than we can fully process, and that attention filters which information makes it into our conscious awareness. That's also true. But because we weren't ready to get into the details, I implied that making it past the gates of attention was a simple yes/no proposition. It's much more nuanced than that. Literally hundreds of discerning scientists are hard at work trying to understand exactly how attention accomplishes its monumental task, and we don't have all the answers. But the filter of attention is definitely more complicated than just a yes/no decision about whether you become aware of something or not. We don't have to go into all the details, but a slightly deeper understanding of how attention works makes a big difference in cultivating mindfulness.

When we pay attention to one thing, we generally remain aware of many other things simultaneously. Even as we hold eye contact during a conversation, we can still perceive some of our surroundings. As we focus on the flavor of our dinner, we can still be aware of ambient sounds in the restaurant. During most of our lives, we remain aware of what we're focused on and also what's in the background. We'll refer to these as the *spotlight of attention* and *peripheral awareness*, respectively.

If we choose to attend to the physical sensations of breathing, we do so by focusing the spotlight of attention on specific sensations like the rise and fall of the chest. This allows us to experience each breath in greater detail. Meanwhile, we nevertheless stay consciously aware of other things in our environment, body, and mind. These things stay in our peripheral awareness.

When you choose an anchor for your attention, your goal is to keep the spotlight of attention focused on your anchor. If you choose an anchor that is narrow—let's say the sensations of breathing at the tip of your nose—then there's only one place the spotlight can shine to stay on your anchor. If instead you choose an anchor that is more broad—let's say any sounds in your environment—then the spotlight of attention is free to dart back and forth between different sounds.

During most tasks in daily life, it's usually necessary for the spotlight to shift back and forth between different aspects of your anchor. While you are driving, your spotlight shifts between the road ahead, your speedometer, your mirrors, and perhaps whatever thoughts happen to be on your mind. When the spotlight lands on your speedometer, you're probably still peripherally aware of the traffic ahead. If the car in front of you stepped on its breaks, you would notice right away and quickly shift your spotlight again. Focusing your attention on one thing doesn't mean shutting out everything else.

To better understand the spotlight of attention and peripheral awareness within the context of mindfulness, it's useful to consider what I call the *continuum of focused attention*. There are four stages, each characterized by a different engagement with your anchor—you can be *absorbed* in your anchor, *focused* on it, *distracted* from it, or *oblivious* to it. To illustrate, let's assume that the chosen anchor for your attention is the breath. At one end of the continuum you are *absorbed*, a state in which the spotlight of attention is vividly focused on only the sensations of the breath and nothing else is in peripheral awareness. This is rare. In the second stage you are *focused*: the breath is in the spotlight of attention and other things are in peripheral awareness. You become *distracted* when something besides the breath is in the spotlight of attention and the breath is in peripheral awareness. Finally, you are *oblivious* when the breath is no longer in the spotlight of attention or peripheral awareness. Oops.

The Continuum of Focused Attention

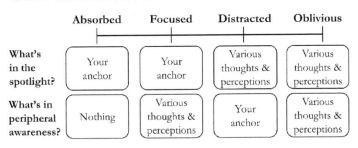

	Absorbed	Focused	Distracted	Oblivious
What's in the spotlight?	Your anchor	Your anchor	Various thoughts & perceptions	Various thoughts & perceptions
What's in peripheral awareness?	Nothing	Various thoughts & perceptions	Your anchor	Various thoughts & perceptions

During meditation, we generally alternate frequently between focus, distraction, and obliviousness. The goal should be to achieve greater levels of focus and fewer instances of being oblivious to your anchor, not to strive for rare states of absorption. Striving for absorption—where there's nothing in your peripheral awareness—is a losing strategy. Can you close your ears? Can you turn off your sense of touch?

To better understand why you shouldn't strive to turn off peripheral awareness, consider what happens when you close your eyes. The darkness that you perceive is not actually the absence of sight. You are seeing blackness. Until recently, I had always assumed that the visual experience of being blind was similar to what I experience when I close my eyes—total blackness. But this isn't always the case. This was memorably illustrated to me by the story of one woman who had been blind throughout her entire life before having her sight partially restored by new advances in medicine. The experience of suddenly being able to see turned out to be quite overwhelming for her, especially because she couldn't turn it off by closing her eyes. Even with her eyes closed, that unfamiliar blackness was still there.

Most of us are so accustomed to that blackness that it doesn't bother us at all. But for this woman, the blackness was intrusive. It disturbed her the way we might get disturbed by the things in our peripheral awareness that we can't turn off—things like discomfort in our bodies or sounds in our environment. But it's possible to learn to relate to these perceptions with the same ease that we experience in response to the darkness of closing our eyes.

Of course, most of us are pretty well acclimated to not only the blackness of closing our eyes but also the constantly shifting content of peripheral awareness in general. We probably don't feel disturbed by most things we hear, see, taste, or smell. It's not until we decide to focus our attention on something specific that the battle with peripheral awareness begins. Suddenly everything around feels like a potential conflict. The sensations in our bodies or the sounds of people around us start being perceived as an obstacle. We may want to shut them all out, but the goal is not to turn off peripheral awareness. That would be impossible. Instead, the goal is to sustain the spotlight of attention on your chosen anchor and allow other thoughts and perceptions to naturally come and go from peripheral awareness. You can remain focused on the sensations of your breath even as the sounds of nearby cars fill your peripheral awareness.

Imagine that you're sitting in a room with many televisions. Each is playing a different channel: touch, taste, sound, sight, smell, feelings, or ideas. While you're awake, all the televisions stay on and each channel plays content most of the time. When you focus your spotlight on any one channel, the volume for that channel gets louder. At the same time, the volume of the other channels may seem to get softer, but they generally won't turn off. If you manage to turn the volume way up on one channel, you may stop noticing the rest of the channels altogether—but turning off channels should not be your goal. You can't deliberately turn off peripheral awareness and trying to do so will make all the inevitable thoughts and perceptions you experience feel like a burden. The goal is to focus on one channel and to let the others simply be as they are without letting them distract you from your anchor.

Understanding the continuum of focused attention—absorbed, focused, distracted, and oblivious—can help us avoid the trap of thinking that mindfulness is about trying to eliminate peripheral awareness. There is a wonderful ease to mindfulness when you understand how to sustain the spotlight of attention on your chosen anchor while allowing other perceptions to float harmlessly in and out of peripheral awareness. Whether hearing loud neighbors as you're trying to fall asleep or waiting in a busy airport to catch your next flight, you can stay focused on your anchor as the endless parade of perceptions drift by without bothering you at all.

6 – THE MISCONCEPTION OF THE QUIET MIND

Perhaps the most widespread misconception about mindfulness is that it requires a still and quiet mind. Many people assume that success in mindfulness is measured by the degree to which you can eliminate distracting thoughts. Let's refer to this as the *misconception of the quiet mind.* It's no wonder that people believe this. After all, mindfulness is often described as a tool to calm the restless chatter of our minds. Plus there are rare states of absorption that do resemble this notion of mindfulness—total stillness of mind undisturbed by thought. Yet the notion that mindfulness requires the absence of thought or distraction is deeply mistaken, and this misunderstanding is among the most important misconceptions to address as someone begins practicing.

Many beginners notice that their minds are completely distracted and then conclude that they are bad at mindfulness and will not benefit from it. This is a bit like saying you're too out of shape to go to the gym. The unspoken logic is that to reap the benefits of mindfulness you have to practice correctly (which is true), and that practicing correctly means having a calm and focused mind (which isn't necessarily true at all). It's an issue of confusing one rather specific goal of meditation—to eventually access states where the mind is completely undistracted for long periods of time—with the actual practice of mindfulness.

The practice of mindfulness is fundamentally about learning how to attend to an anchor and release distractions. Your skill in releasing is developed one distraction at a time, and it takes many thousands of times to get good at it. Without distraction, you couldn't practice. Similar to how you might complete repetitions of an exercise at the gym, you can think about mindfulness practice as having a fundamental repetition: (1) you focus your attention on a chosen anchor like the sensations of your breath, (2) distraction arises, (3) you notice the distraction, and (4) you release the distraction. Then you return back to step one, focusing your attention on the anchor. One repetition at a time, you develop the ability to avoid getting swept away by distraction.

Everyone experiences some level of distraction when they begin practicing mindfulness, and it's not important whether your level is high or low. Imagine that while practicing mindfulness you were to get distracted every few seconds, but you always noticed it quickly and then earnestly returned your attention back to your anchor. Many people would feel frustrated with this experience and interpret it as a failure. However, the opposite is true. This experience would actually be quite beneficial—and even impressive—because of the consistency with which you noticed distractions and released them. Distraction is inevitable. If you interpret it as a problem, you will likely become frustrated and lose motivation. It is crucial to see distraction as an opportunity to practice letting go. Repetition by repetition, we develop the powerful skills of attending and releasing one distraction at a time.

Part II:

THOUGHTS, EVALUATIONS, & EMOTIONS

7 – THE NATURE OF THOUGHTS

Our own thoughts can be salient distractions while we're practicing mindfulness. The mind generates thoughts spontaneously, and trying to suppress them usually backfires. It is well-documented that trying to suppress a thought can ironically lead to a greater occurrence of that very thought. Just try to avoid thinking about a white bear. Seriously, try it. Think about whatever else you want, just don't let a white bear come to mind.

Okay, what just happened? Most likely, trying to suppress the thought of a white bear made you think of it. Even if for a little while you could keep it at bay by focusing on something else—pink flamingo, pink flamingo, pink flamingo—as soon as you let up, in rushes that bear. The best way to avoid thinking about a white bear is to simply release the thought and focus elsewhere, rather than actively trying to prevent the thought from ever arising. This difference between suppressing versus releasing a thought is subtle, but it is a crucial distinction in the practice of mindfulness. Suppressing a thought involves trying to prevent it from arising. That's a nearly impossible task that mostly creates tension. By contrast, releasing a thought involves choosing not to elaborate the thought once it has arisen.

Even though we can't necessarily control how thoughts arise, we can choose whether we pay attention to them. Most of us have a strong tendency to elaborate an initial idea into a long train of thought (*my foot is falling asleep…my professor said that happens because of a harmless blockage of nerve signals, not blood shortage…I can't believe I got a B+ in that class…etc.*). By the time we realize that we are distracted, we often can't even remember how we got so off track.

Mindfulness teaches us how to avoid getting lost in extended trains of thought. We don't have to view thoughts as the enemy, and we also don't have to get caught up in each one that comes by. Instead, we can treat thoughts like cars passing by on a road. The goal isn't to stop traffic, but to watch it pass by without getting in one of the cars.

Learning to release rather than elaborate thoughts takes considerable practice. Part of the challenge is that we tend to take thoughts very seriously. Thinking can of course be useful, but we have an unconscious tendency to exaggerate the importance of thoughts in three key ways.

First, even though we may understand intellectually that thoughts are transient, we still slip into relating to thoughts as though they were enduring. This gives them an appearance of solidity and significance even though they are actually ephemeral. Unless we elaborate thoughts, they are powerless because they disappear almost as soon as they appear.

Second, we view thoughts as inherently accurate descriptions of reality. Every thought arrives in our mind with the implicit message that it is true, even though we of course shouldn't believe everything we think.

29

Third, we view thoughts as direct representations of who we are as a person. This dramatically raises the stakes, linking our thoughts to our sense of personal identity. Yet who you are as a person is so much more than the thoughts you experience, many of which flicker across your mind with little consequence and no real ability to define you as a person.

We might not consciously describe thoughts in these three ways, but we probably still find ourselves relating to them as though they are lasting, inherently true, and deeply personal. The actual nature of thoughts is quite different, and sometimes this is easiest to see in other people's experiences. When someone seems to constantly change their mind, it's easy to see how fleeting thoughts can be. When someone falsely accuses us, it's painfully obvious that thoughts are not direct windows into reality. And if a young child were to feel like a bad person for having a hostile thought, we wouldn't nod our heads disapprovingly and agree with them. It's easy to reassure a kid that they are not defined by the thoughts that pop into their minds.

It's also possible to see the true nature of thoughts in our own experience if we spend some time examining them. For instance, have you ever watched a scary movie and then wanted to avoid thinking about it later? I remember lying in bed as a kid after watching a horror flick and desperately trying to avoid any thoughts about it. I was in my own bed in a locked house in a safe neighborhood, literally afraid of a thought. This is an extreme but illustrative example of how we view thoughts as meaningful and important things with serious consequences. At the time, I didn't have the perspective to realize that it didn't matter what thought popped into my mind. I was safe, and any scary thoughts that did arise could pass away just as quickly.

Recognizing the transient, subjective, and even impersonal nature of thoughts helps break their spell, making it easier to avoid getting caught up in any given thought. This is sometimes described as a process of *decentering*. It involves taking thoughts down from a false pedestal and seeing them for what they truly are. When we recognize thoughts as fleeting, subjective, and impersonal, they don't hold such power over our minds. We no longer take every thought so seriously, which makes it much easier to release the ones that don't serve us.

8 – HARNESSING THE THINKING MIND

Thoughts are transient, subjective, and impersonal, but the right thought can change the world if you know how to run with it. Fortunately, having the ability to release thoughts doesn't mean that we must forfeit the value of thinking. Recalling the past, anticipating the future, and thinking things through are among the most valuable human capacities. We can use these abilities to improve our quality of life and to benefit others, and abandoning them would be deeply misguided. Yet at the same time, few of us engage our thinking minds in a remotely optimal way. For many of us, recollection, anticipation, and analysis are invaluable skills that have gone rogue. They are like power tools—helpful at the right time and place, but not if they are running every moment of the day. The last thing you need is a jackhammer whirling away while you try to enjoy dinner with your family or fall asleep at night.

How much of your thinking is actually useful? Few of us have the self-awareness to accurately answer this question. Our minds generate thousands of thoughts every day, yet we take stock of only a small proportion of these. This is easily revealed by attempting to observe every thought that arises for even just ten minutes. If you try this, you will likely discover that thoughts rush endlessly through your mind. If even a small proportion of these were truly useful, your mind would be a place of awe inspiring innovation and efficiency. In reality, our thoughts are only occasionally worthwhile. By learning to release the thoughts that are unnecessary or destructive, we can have much more productive minds.

Just as importantly, how much of your thinking is truly beneficial to your state of mind? Research into mind-wandering suggests that only a small fraction of people's thoughts are pleasant—and even when thinking about something pleasant we tend to be no happier than when we are simply present with what we are doing. Instead, people are on average more likely to have neutral or unpleasant thoughts, and these are associated with greater unhappiness. It's not that thinking is inherently at odds with happiness, it's just that most people are at the mercy of their mind's habitual tendency to think about things that stress them out.

Some people worry that practicing mindfulness will require that they stop planning for the future, reminiscing about the past, and daydreaming in pleasant or productive ways. Giving up all those things would be silly. The goal is not to decommission the thinking mind. The goal is to use the powerful tools of the thinking mind in the right way and at the right times. Mindfulness actually makes us better at thinking because we can use the skills of attending and releasing to direct our train of thought towards productive and helpful ends. We not only learn to more quickly release the thoughts that are unhelpful, but it gets easier to elaborate the thoughts that are truly worthwhile. In this way, it opens up more mental bandwidth while also helping us use that bandwidth more efficiently. Over time we can learn to engage our thinking minds in a more skillful way and at the most opportune times.

9 – EVALUATION & THE CONDITIONS FOR OUR HAPPINESS

Our tendency to evaluate what we experience is so pervasive that we often don't even recognize we are doing it. Almost as quickly as we notice something, we evaluate it. *Do I like this? Is this good? Is this true?* We eat a food and immediately judge its flavor as tasty or unappetizing. We might say something in an important meeting and immediately judge it as smart or stupid. Even our conversations with others are often driven by sharing our evaluations. If you keep a look out for it, you will quickly notice how predominant evaluation is in your life from moment to moment.

Evaluations are more than just a description. They are judgments about something's value or worth. Saying that a food tastes sweet is a *description*. Saying that it tastes delicious is an *evaluation*. We might judge something as being true or false, attractive or ugly, strong or weak—all of which carry a connotation of something's value. Ultimately, many evaluations boil down to whether we like something or not.

From one perspective, it seems reasonable to constantly

make evaluations. In principle, we evaluate everything that is happening to us so that we can respond appropriately. If food tastes good, it's safe to eat more. If it tastes rotten, better to avoid it. Evaluation itself isn't a problem. It's an essential capacity that allows us to effectively navigate the world around us. When we judge an experience in a way that is both accurate and beneficial, the evaluation is skillful. It makes our lives better. When our judgments are inaccurate or harmful, they are unskillful. They make our lives worse. Ideally, evaluation helps us develop *discernment:* an accurate understanding of consequences that helps us know what to do in order to most benefit ourselves and those we care about.

Yet just like the capacity to think about the past and the future, the ability to evaluate can go awry. We can—and often do—make evaluations that serve no real purpose. Worse yet, we often get entangled in unskillful evaluations that make life more difficult. A huge amount of our unhappiness stems from negative evaluations of our circumstances. A long line at the grocery store becomes a tremendous inconvenience. A blemish on our face becomes a nagging insecurity. We attribute our dissatisfaction to the long line or blemish, not recognizing that our evaluations are the real source of our suffering.

Our happiness in life depends less on our circumstances than on how we evaluate them. We observe this every time we see two people have completely different reactions to the same situation. Every time it rains, some people are frustrated while others enjoy it. The circumstances are shared, but the experience depends on each person's evaluation.

I witnessed this in a memorable way when having dinner one evening with a friend at his home. We were dining in his garden on a beautiful night just as the sun was setting. The sky was full of color, the air was warm, the food had been carefully prepared, and we had no nagging responsibilities to prevent us from enjoying the evening together. It was one of those rare moments when everything comes together to create a moment you want to savor, yet somehow my friend seemed intent on missing it. His attention was pulled to the leaves that had fallen unwelcomed to his lawn and various little improvements he wanted to make to his backyard. Out of everything happening in that moment, his attention was focused on the few things that seemed out of place. His evaluation of these things as problems overshadowed the joy that he could have been experiencing on that otherwise beautiful evening. I often think of that dinner to remind myself that we can allow the conditions necessary for our happiness to become unnecessarily narrow. We can usually find something to be unhappy about even when things are going particularly well.

On the other side of the continuum, evaluation also plays a huge role in how we find resilience and meaning during even life's most difficult challenges. Dr. Viktor Frankl—who survived three years in a concentration camp during the Holocaust—famously observed, "Everything can be taken from a man but one thing: the last of human freedoms—to choose one's attitude in any given set of circumstances." The ultimate power we have is choosing what an experience means to us, which we accomplish by choosing how we evaluate that experience.

Your evaluations have the power to make the best out of the worst situation or the worst out of the best situation. Personally, I consider this good news. It means that there's a way to make our experience of life much better simply by reconsidering the way we view our circumstances. Fortunately, mindfulness helps us to become more aware of the evaluations that we make and the consequences they have. With practice, we can also become better at releasing counterproductive evaluations and fostering those that are actually beneficial. This needs to be guided by discernment. We have to learn which evaluations to abandon and which to cultivate. Mindfully observing our own experiences helps create this discernment, but we can also learn from other people's experience and wisdom. A good place to begin is reflecting on the various ways that evaluation tends to go awry. That's the topic of the next two chapters.

10 – THE VIOLENCE OF COMPARISON

As we've discussed, the conditions necessary for our happiness can become overly narrow. One way this happens is in our need to have more than others. Humans have a strong tendency to evaluate most things in life by comparing them to other things, but it is unlikely I have to tell you that. Psychologists sometimes call this the *positional bias:* we're often less concerned with our absolute circumstances than in how our circumstances compare to those around us. Many of us now enjoy the luxuries of soft beds, abundant food, and constant access to unparalleled information and entertainment—unimaginable luxuries to humans living thousands of years ago. Yet despite this abundance, we slip into dissatisfaction by comparing our circumstances to what others have or what we *could* have. If we scratch our new car, the scratch is a trivial deviation in our absolute circumstances. We still have a new car, gas to fuel it, roads to drive, and places worth going. Yet having the scratch feels worse than not having the scratch an hour ago—and relatively worse than all the other cars with perfectly smooth and sculpted bumpers.

Relative evaluations are not inherently a problem. They can be accurate, and they are often productive and useful. Both my personal and professional life require making relative comparisons every day, such as delegating a project by identifying the best person for the job. Relative evaluations can also fill us with a sense of gratitude if we reflect on how much better our circumstances must be relative to most of our human ancestors. And even upward social comparisons—when we look to those who have what we want—can sometimes inspire and motivate us to make more out of our lives (more on this later).

Nevertheless, there's a dark side to making relative comparisons that we would be wise to recognize and confront. For example, social comparisons sometimes strain our relationships and self-worth. Men report lower relationship satisfaction after exposure to highly attractive females, as women do after exposure to highly dominant men. When exposed to attractive members of the same sex, we rate ourselves as less worth marrying. Simply by seeing photos of highly attractive people, we feel more insecure. This dilemma is only getting worse in the digital era. Increasingly, people are exposed almost constantly to airbrushed celebrities or posts on social networks that highlight only the best parts of acquaintances' lives. The default human response to all this is to feel a little worse about oneself.

Although a competitive spirit has its place in life, the positional bias often generates an underlying motive to be better than others that can become the undercurrent of our entire lives. Ultimately, this sets up a losing battle. It's a zero-sum game, meaning that for one person to win someone else must lose.

No matter how hard we strive, we certainly can't be the

best at everything. This means that we can always count on there being someone who is more wealthy, attractive, or intelligent. It's inevitable, and the positional bias leads us to interpret it as a problem. Even when we do succeed at having more than others, we often find that our satisfaction is fleeting because our comparison group and standards change as well. Every achievement brings us closer to a receding horizon, until one day we wake up in a panic wondering whether our two-bedroom yacht will look a little *small* to our new friends in the Dubai Marina.

The zero-sum nature of the positional bias also makes it difficult to take genuine joy in the success of others. I've witnessed this all too often within academia in the half-hearted congratulations offered to colleagues when they publish in top journals or secure big grants. Although we're usually at least a little happy for others, it's easy to slip into relative comparison and feel somehow less worthy when others succeed. This not only dampens the other person's enjoyment and obstructs an opportunity to deepen our relationship with them, but is also a missed opportunity to increase the joy in our own lives. If we only rejoice at our own success, our celebrations are fairly limited. If we can find joy in others' achievements, there is no limit to our happiness.

When I was in high school, I read an article in a men's magazine on how to most effectively compliment a woman. The advice was simple: tell her she is better than other people she knows. Tell her she is the most beautiful of all her friends. Tell her she has a better sense of style than anyone else in the office. As a young kid, I was impressed by the simplicity and power of this strategy—even if part of me knew that it looked ripe but was rotten inside. I started noticing these compliments everywhere. One night driving back from my then girlfriend's ballet performance, her mom told her that she was more poised than any of her friends on stage. I knew her friends, of course. I was glad they weren't in the car.

The positional bias is fundamentally about comparison, and comparisons are usually made at someone's expense. I call this *the violence of comparison*—not to imply a physical violence, but to highlight the power that comparisons have to hurt us. Even a heartfelt compliment can have unintended consequences when it is formed as a relative evaluation. When we want to offer someone a meaningful compliment, it is natural to want to tell them how much they stand out from others. After all, one of the most gratifying compliments to receive is being told that we are *the best*. These words speak to the part of each of us that needs reassurance and that thinks in terms of the positional bias. But when someone is the best, all others must be relatively worse. A compliment to one person can inadvertently be a criticism to many others. Even for the recipient, this kind of compliment can reinforce the tendency to think in terms of relative position—perpetuating the implicit belief that our value depends on being better than others.

We certainly make comparisons at the expense of others, but often the violence of comparison gets directed at ourselves. It shows up whenever we compare ourselves to those who have something we want. One reason the violence of comparison can be so problematic is that we often make highly selective comparisons to only certain aspects of another person. This was memorably illustrated to me by one woman's experience in a yoga class. She would find the one person in the room with leaner arms than her and feel insecure by comparison. She would also find the one person in the room with a better downward facing dog. And the one with a more stylish outfit. In a room full of people, it's easy to find at least

42

one person with more flexible hamstrings. From an outside perspective, we can see that these perceived inferiorities are really not a big deal. Yet because the positional bias is deeply ingrained in our thinking, we can get trapped in dissatisfaction anytime anyone has more than we do. The reality is that someone is always going to have more.

The positional bias is a natural part of the human mind, but we don't have to resign ourselves to letting social comparisons limit our happiness. We can use mindfulness to become aware of the comparisons we make, see their consequences more clearly, and choose which evaluations we want to attend to and which we want to release. For a couple years of my life, this was one of the most transformative aspects of my mindfulness practice. My wife and I made a game out of catching ourselves every time one of us made a comparison. There was a subtle violence to most of the comparisons I made, and it was remarkable how completely unnecessary most of them were. They were pointless, but not harmless. So I made a habit of noting the comparison and then releasing it by not giving it any more attention. Immediately, the act of releasing comparisons made them less powerful. Without endorsement or elaboration, the comparisons couldn't perpetuate my dissatisfaction or insecurity. And over time, I started making fewer unnecessary comparisons.

As the positional bias is slowly losing its power over me, comparisons now come to mind less often. When they do, I can usually choose to engage or release them depending on whether they seem accurate and useful. Looking back now with a little perspective, I can see that much of the suffering I experienced from social comparisons over the years was ultimately self-inflicted. It was like the positional bias was holding my wrist and slapping me with my own hand. But no one teased, "Why are you hitting yourself, Mike?" so I just assumed that the blows were an inevitable consequence of not being as good as others.

11 – SELF-CRITICISM & JUDGMENT LOOPS

The violence of comparison is part of a broader theme of self-criticism that is an enormous misuse of the capacity for evaluation. We are capable of judging anyone or anything, but many people judge themselves most of all. We get caught up in self-criticism, treating ourselves in a way we would never allow others to treat us. If a friend started criticizing us the way that many of us criticize ourselves, we would be deeply offended. Although we wouldn't tolerate it from someone else, many of us live with a chronic stream of self-criticism that we simply accept.

Sometimes we accept this level of self-criticism because we slip into viewing it as the unquestionable truth. We don't stop to question its validity. When someone else tells us something, we typically evaluate whether we think it's true. But for thoughts that are self-generated, we rarely apply this same degree of skepticism. We simply accept our thoughts as true by default. This is why meditation teachers are constantly telling their students *don't believe everything you think*.

One young woman I had been coaching each week for a year finally told me about a deep insecurity she had about the shape of her eyes. As a child, some friends had briefly teased her about it and she had internalized the insult as a fundamental truth. From then on, her insecurity came to mind whenever she walked into a room of new people. I had been staring at her face for over a year, and the thought that her eyes were in any way unusual had never crossed my mind. She was beautiful. Yet each day for the past ten years she perpetuated the self-criticism.

We all have insecurities, and most people feel like those insecurities are grounded in real, objective, unflattering facts about who they are. It's true that you're not perfect. But it's also true that many of our self-criticisms are exaggerated and unnecessary evaluations based on flimsy assumptions. Like most thoughts, self-critical evaluations pop into our minds with the underlying message that they are inherently true. We tend to believe our negative evaluations as though their mere existence were proof of their validity. Even when we do half-heartedly attempt to question the validity of our self-criticisms, we rarely give ourselves the gift of true perspective—something I know all too well from experience. I've been skinny my entire life, even though I've often wished I weren't. At times when a quiet voice of wisdom questioned whether being so thin was actually a problem, I've been able to watch a lawyerly rebuttal quickly come to mind in the criticism's defense: "Remember the time that girl innocently said you looked like a normal person who had just been stretched out to be taller? Proof!". Never mind that I can run, jump, swim, and win the heart of the girl of my dreams. It really is a serious problem. Right?

One particularly challenging form of self-criticism is when

we get caught in self-perpetuating cycles of negative evaluations. I call these judgment loops, and there are two closely related types. The first type is when an *event* leads to a *negative evaluation*, which leads to an *emotion*, which leads to another *event* that perpetuates the cycle. Imagine that you glance at yourself in the mirror (*the event*), become convinced some part of your body is unattractive (*the evaluation*), and feel ashamed as a consequence (*the emotion*). Already the experience is unpleasant, though it would be short-lived if you released the evaluation and moved on (more on this in the next chapter). But instead, you walk to the mirror and take a closer look, reaffirm your initial evaluation, and feel even worse. Maybe eventually you even feel badly enough that you choose to distract yourself with an unhealthy snack, which elicits even more self-criticism, which makes you feel even worse. Everyone's trap is different, but most everyone gets stuck in these self-perpetuating cycles sometimes.

This kind of destructive judgment loop can also happen between people. Imagine someone says something critical of you (*the event*), you perceive it as disrespectful (*the evaluation*), and you get angry (*the emotion*). So your body language closes off (*the event*), they perceive you as being upset with them (*the evaluation*), and they get defensive (*the emotion*). Now everyone's emotions are causing them to give off less than ideal signals (*the event*), which both people quickly evaluate as evidence of the other person's wrongdoing (*the evaluation*), leading to even greater levels of anger and defensiveness (*the emotion*). Let the descending cycle of poor communication begin!

A second type of judgment loop is even more challenging. It occurs when we begin to make negative evaluations of our *emotions* that only deepen those same emotions. In this scenario, the event is the emotion itself. For example, you feel ashamed because of how you evaluate your body, and then you make a negative evaluation of your shame which makes you feel even worse. The shame about your shame about your shame keeps accumulating until something breaks the pattern. I see this all the time in those who are struggling with depression or anxiety. Being depressed is evaluated as a failure, which only deepens the depression. Our negative evaluations of the emotions themselves just exacerbate the same emotions.

How do we get out of these judgment loops? Ultimately, we have to release the evaluations that are perpetuating them. That's where mindfulness can make all the difference. We'll discuss how the skills of attending and releasing can help us address unskillful habits of evaluation in the next chapter.

12 – RELEASING UNSKILLFUL EVALUATIONS

By now it should be clear that we all make evaluations that are unhelpful. There is no way to stop making counterproductive evaluations out of sheer force of will, but there is also no need to endorse or elaborate every evaluation that pops into our minds. Like any other thought that bubbles to the surface, we can simply release the evaluations that don't serve us. These unskillful evaluations are often unfavorable judgments of ourselves or our circumstances, but favorable evaluations can also be problematic. I work at a university where a surprising number of students view getting black-out drunk favorably. A positive evaluation of your ninth shot—which may spend longer in the toilet than in your stomach—is probably not the greatest help.

One benefit of releasing unskillful evaluations is that it can lead to a greater acceptance of things as they are. Acceptance involves experiencing what is present in any given moment without wanting it to be different, which generally requires letting go of the negative evaluations of our circumstances. Acceptance makes sense when a negative evaluation of our circumstances would be false, counterproductive, or unnecessary. We can safely accept our receding hairline, but it would be dangerous to accept an abusive spouse. Acceptance can also be helpful when circumstances are truly beyond our control, helping us avoid unnecessary distress over things that we cannot change. Yet there can be uncertainty in whether our negative evaluations are helpful or whether we have the control to change our circumstances. As the serenity prayer highlights, discernment must guide this process: *Grant me the serenity to accept the things I cannot change, the courage to change the things I can, and the wisdom to know the difference.*

There is no simple way to know which evaluations we should embrace and which we should release. True wisdom takes time to develop. Mindfulness can accelerate this process because it gives us much greater familiarity with our minds, including the consequences of the evaluations we make. Mindfulness can help us see that aversion to our circumstances often causes even more suffering than the circumstances themselves. We see this easily in a child distraught over a harmless game, though it is harder to recognize in our own quiet distress over the shape of our bodies. Still, it's usually not hard to identify at least some habitual patterns of evaluation that don't serve us. That is the low-hanging fruit. Start there.

Some people are reluctant to release even the negative evaluations that make them unhappy because they fear losing the motivation that springs from that dissatisfaction. They worry that releasing upward social comparisons or dissatisfaction with their current circumstances might lead to a life devoid of aspiration. The logic is that these negative evaluations are necessary to stay motivated to improve. Of course, the approach we take to evaluation doesn't need to be an all-or-none proposition. The goal isn't to abandon evaluation—if an evaluation is truly serving you, there's no need to change it. Yet it's important to recognize that social comparisons and negative evaluations of our circumstances are not the only, or even the best, sources of motivation. For one thing, they sometimes create more stress and distraction than lasting motivation. They tend to put us in a worse mood, which isn't the state most conducive to high motivation and effective work. Furthermore, our upward social comparisons can also trigger insecurity, which compromises our ability to approach and interact comfortably with the people who most inspire us. But most importantly, it's a dangerous mindset to assume that motivation is incompatible with contentment. It mistakenly puts two crucial elements of a life well-lived in direct conflict. Even those who thoroughly enjoy their lives and feel no need to compare themselves to others can still find good reasons to learn and grow—perhaps most enduringly by an aspiration to improve the lives of others.

Throughout much of my own life, I drew great motivation from unfavorable evaluations of my circumstances. Still today, I can be quick to identify a problem and launch into action to resolve it. But as many of my habitual negative evaluations have fallen away and a greater contentment has rushed to take its place, I find myself as motivated as ever. Even without feeling that anything is missing from my life—or perhaps precisely for that reason—I am able to set my sights on ever greater aspirations that extend beyond securing my own personal happiness.

One reason it's easy to stay motivated is that I've cultivated new evaluations that sustain my drive—like choosing to evaluate hard work as rewarding. For much of my life, I viewed hard work as a necessary burden. This evaluation made work fell like a chore, which made it difficult to stay intrinsically motivated. By choosing to reframe work as a way to make a positive contribution to the lives of other people, hard work started to feel more like a rewarding opportunity. In this way, we can use mindfulness to not only release unskillful judgments as they arise, but also to be proactive in cultivating new evaluations to take their place.

As another example, I've found it helpful to foster a new interpretation of the physiological changes I experience before a big speech. Throughout most of my life, I evaluated a racing heart before a presentation as a signal of problematic anxiety. This of course only increased my worry. Eventually I learned that this stress response was actually helping prepare my body to perform—increasing my energy, focusing my mind, and even helping me think a bit faster. So I chose to start cultivating a different interpretation of the experience. I accepted that I was feeling anxiety, but I also started recognizing that there was an important purpose to the changes in my body. So when my heart started racing, I would direct my mind to the more empowering interpretation of what it signified. I wasn't abandoning the truth for a comforting story, but instead broadening my perspective in a way that made my experience of the anxiety less aversive. This strategy of cultivating a new evaluation is called *reappraisal,* and it's something we'll discuss at length in the context of emotion within the next few chapters.

13 – UNDERSTANDING EMOTIONS

At this point, you're familiar with how to use the skills of attending and releasing to influence your thoughts and evaluations. Now it's time to start applying what you've learned to your emotions. After all, what we *feel* is one of the most important things in life. If you push people to explain why they want the things they want, it often boils down to the way it will make them feel. We want a stable job to have money, we want money to have financial security, and we want financial security so we can live without fear. Given that so much of our time is devoted to activities that we pursue because of how we hope they will make us feel, it certainly makes sense to take some time to learn how to work with emotions more directly.

Our emotions also matter because they so strongly shape our thinking and behavior. Emotions are like puppeteers that influence both our psychology and our body's physiology in intricate ways. The specific pattern of physiology, thought, and behavior that is encouraged by each emotion has evolved over time because it tended to help our ancestors deal with certain repeated challenges. Imagine that you're walking alone late at night in a bad part of town and you notice that a group of men are following you. As they get closer, you may become afraid—and quickly many changes occur in your body and mind. Your heart likely starts racing to circulate greater levels of blood to muscles that might soon be needed. Your sole priority becomes avoiding the immediate threat, and any other goals you might have been pursuing are suddenly irrelevant. In turn, your attention narrows to just the potential threat and any means of escape. Your mind is also directed to thoughts that might be relevant—a distant memory of a self-defense class comes to mind, but definitely not that painting class you took years ago.

When you experience intense fear, it can profoundly shape your entire experience of life in that moment. Other emotions have distinct but powerful effects as well. Falling in love makes us elated, overriding our other concerns and locking us away from life's hassles behind closed bedroom doors. Even when emotions are not particularly strong, they still influence us in important ways. In fact, the people close to us sometimes have an easier time than we do at noticing how our moods are subtly shaping our behavior. My wife knows within seconds of my walking in the door if something is wrong. Even a small lingering frustration with a project at work can subtly change our body language, eye contact, tone of voice, and conversational style when we're home with family.

Emotions make our bodies and minds click into specific patterns of thought, physiology, and behavior that can often be helpful, but that doesn't mean that the emotions we experience are always good for us. Fortunately, mindfulness gives us greater awareness of our emotions as well as greater choice over how we relate to them. With practice, mindfulness can dramatically improve our emotional lives in several ways. In the next few chapters, we'll discuss how mindfulness helps us relate effectively to challenging emotions, dismantle destructive emotions, and even cultivate the positive emotions that can make life so sweet.

14 - WILLINGNESS

Mindfulness is not about eliminating emotions from your life. Naturally, most people prefer to avoid difficult emotions like fear, sadness, or anger. Yet even difficult emotions have their place in life. So although we will discuss strategies for deliberately influencing which emotions we experience, it's helpful to start by recognizing that sometimes our inclination to avoid negative emotions can backfire. When we view emotions as a burden, our negative evaluation of them often creates even more suffering. We struggle over the struggle. Being more willing to experience emotions can help us discover a new way of relating to them.

This *willingness* to experience a difficult emotion is actually a hallmark of mindfulness. Willingness means allowing an emotion to exist without trying to change it. This requires releasing the evaluation that a difficult emotion is a problem. Unpleasant emotions are a natural and inevitable part of life, and they don't have to be a threat. Mindfulness has increased the range of emotions that I'm willing to experience, in part because I'm no longer afraid that I'll lose control over them.

Willingness becomes much easier when we learn to decenter from emotions by recognizing them as transient and impersonal—just as we decenter from thoughts by recognizing their true nature. Even those emotions that seem to dominate our lives are constantly ebbing and flowing. By their very nature, they simply cannot be permanent. Recognizing the transient nature of emotions makes it easier to experience them without an accompanying heaviness, urgency, or dread. Given that emotions are transient, they also can't truly define us. Emotions feel so central to our experience that it is easy to slip into thinking that they define who we are as a person, but we are so much more than our shifting emotions.

Both the transient and impersonal nature of emotions have been illustrated to me during the first two years of my daughter's life. She can fluctuate from pure joy to frustration and back again within a single minute. It has been fascinating to see how easily I can slip into defining her based on the emotions she has been experiencing most predominantly. Others often do this too, remarking either how angelic or willful she is as a person based on their recent observations of her emotions. Based on this generalization, they then make predictions about what our lives will be like with that kind of child. Of course, the truth is that our girl is at times angelic, at times willful, and at times she is dozens of other ways. Characterizing her based on a recent pattern of emotion is to neglect the complexity and fluidity of who she is as a person. The same is true for ourselves. It's natural to identify very strongly with our emotions, but it's helpful to remember that even those emotions that we experience most frequently still make up only a small part of who we are.

Having greater perspective about the nature of emotions makes it easier to allow them to be part of our experience.

With practice, we can take a step further and respond to difficult emotions with a welcoming attitude. As counterintuitive as this may sound, it's a powerful strategy that is particularly helpful for emotions that persist even when they are not being perpetuated by our conscious thoughts and evaluations. This sometimes happens to me before I speak to a large audience. I feel anxiety and get a strong shot of adrenaline, which likely stems from an underlying fear of not performing well enough (whatever that means). Even when I consciously focus on the opportunity to help someone in the audience or on the obvious fact that the health and happiness of my family don't hinge on my performance, the anxiety will sometimes persist. In these moments, I find the most helpful thing to do is to be fully willing to be anxious. I welcome the anxiety, resist the default evaluation that it's a problem, and allow myself to experience it as fully as possible. Because I'm no longer in conflict with the emotion, it becomes less threatening. I may still feel anxious, but I also reconnect with the fact that I'm fundamentally okay even with the anxiety.

To be concrete, how exactly do we practice willingness? Reading this chapter and reflecting on the nature of emotions is helpful, but then what? Often the first step is to simply notice whether we have a tendency to evaluate our emotions as problematic. This evaluation can happen so quickly and automatically that we don't even realize that it's happening. When we do notice that we're evaluating an emotion as a problem, we can try to release that evaluation. You won't be an expert at this the first time you try. It will take practice, and it's easiest to begin with emotions that don't feel overwhelming. Sometimes it also helps to take a moment to remind yourself that emotions are ultimately fleeting and impersonal. We can also try to remember that we are still okay even if we're experiencing something difficult. Taking these steps can help us drop the automatic impulse to immediately try to change or eliminate the emotion.

If you find it difficult to be willing to experience an emotion, sometimes it helps to watch the emotion closely to get a better understanding of it. Over time, this investigation can lead to an experience of decentering from the emotion. For instance, you could attend to the physiological changes in your body, any pleasantness or unpleasantness, and especially the shifting and fleeting nature of the emotion. This kind of investigation can make the constantly changing emotional landscape of our lives a process of exploration and discovery rather than one of resistance and struggle.

A willingness to experience our own emotions helps us let others experience their emotions as well. People rarely want someone to try to change their emotional experience, even when it's painful. Perhaps the most widespread relationship advice—often given to men but relevant to everyone—is to listen to your partner's challenges without immediately trying to fix them. This isn't easy advice to follow, partly because we naturally want to help but also because of the emotions we experience when listening to someone else. Whether we feel empathy, impatience, or defensiveness, it's not uncommon to want to change how someone else feels in order to address our own emotional experience. Although it's not easy—and approaches black belt levels of mastery in our most intimate relationships—it's a powerful skill to be able to allow our emotions to unfold naturally as we create a space for someone else to do the same.

A willingness to experience our own emotions also helps us to be able to share our experience with others. Emotions weave through every day of our lives, but many people are reluctant to speak openly about them. Challenging emotions in particular are treated as mostly private affairs, and the painful ones are often wrapped in shame. So we keep emotions to ourselves and try to come up with our own strategies for managing them, which is about the slowest and least reliable path to emotional mastery. Looking back over my life there were so many times I wish I had the courage and wisdom to have shared my emotional life more openly so I could have learned how to work with those feelings more effectively. I can still vividly remember when as a kid I went through a long spell of loneliness and insecurity after suddenly losing my closest friends. Even at that young age, I didn't want my peers or even my family to know the extent of my sadness. So I carried—and unintentionally perpetuated—what seemed like an unshakeable burden of heavy emotion. If I had been more willing to experience the insecurity, I think I would have been more willing to express it. Then it wouldn't have been a secret burden, but instead an opportunity for connection to my family and a chance to learn more about myself and my emotions.

15 – WORKING WITH DIFFICULT EMOTIONS

Some say that the willingness to simply witness emotions without trying to change them is *the* mindful approach to all emotions, though I disagree. That's a valuable strategy, but there is no single approach that applies to all emotions in all contexts. There are also helpful strategies that use mindfulness to proactively reduce destructive emotions and cultivate positive emotions.

Although most people think emotions are things that happen *to* them, where we choose to focus our attention and the meaning that we give to events are the strongest causes of what we feel. I didn't appreciate this as a teenager when my family moved across the country and uprooted me from my childhood home. After years of shifting social dynamics, I had finally found a group of friends I cherished as well as my first serious girlfriend. Just as my life was coming together, my parents made the brilliant decision to move us half way across the country to Minnesota—a place that gets so cold that on some winter nights your spit will literally freeze before hitting the ground. We arrived to our new home in advance of our furniture on the night before my junior year of high school. That night, I wrestled with resentment and sadness as I tried to fall asleep on the floor. The next morning as I walked into my new school, the emotion had transformed into fear, loneliness, and insecurity. I ate lunch in the stairwell for several days during the first weeks, in part to try to avoid the self-consciousness involved in constantly trying to forge new friendships. I also didn't want my new peers to sense my anxiety. Through all this, there was a distinct sense that all of this hardship—including the uncomfortable emotions I was experiencing—was happening *to* me.

As it turned out, one of my closest childhood friends had given me a book about mindfulness just before I moved. I had no idea what mindfulness was, but I read for ten minutes before going to sleep each night. Although my days were filled with so many difficult emotions, something unexpected would happen each night. I would read, close my eyes, and actually fall asleep feeling happy. When I noticed this pattern, a lightbulb went off in my mind. The unexpected happiness showed me just how much my emotional life was determined by where my mind was focused. I recognized that the painful emotions that I experienced all day were being perpetuated in large part by what I was focusing on and the way I was choosing to evaluate my circumstances. Although it took me many more years to become truly effective at using mindfulness to relate to my emotions, this insight nevertheless made a huge difference for me during that transition. It helped me learn to face the challenges of starting a new life without ruminating on everything that I had lost. In reclaiming my focus, I began reclaiming my emotional well-being.

You'll recall that mindfulness isn't about trying to

suppress thoughts, but instead learning how to choose which thoughts to elaborate and which to release. We can relate to emotions in a similar way. The duration of an emotion depends crucially on where you focus your attention. Many emotions last only seconds or minutes unless we keep focusing on the things that are fueling that emotion. For example, have you ever gotten sad or angry because someone criticized you? The initial emotional reaction to criticism doesn't actually last very long, but we often replay the criticism a hundred times in our minds. By perpetuating the criticism over and over, we fuel the emotion and allow it to continue.

Even the most powerful forest fire usually starts with just a small spark. If you light a match and drop it in an empty parking lot, the match will go out by itself. If you drop that same match in the middle of a dry forest, you'll create an inferno. Many of us have habitual patterns of thoughts and evaluations that strongly predispose us to certain emotions— it's as if we are walking around with minds full of kindling, and even a little spark can set us ablaze. Then once we're in the midst of a strong emotion, we often respond by throwing gas on the fire without even realizing that we're doing it. Our thoughts and evaluations act as fuel that keep emotions burning. The more fuel we give a fire, the bigger it gets and the longer it lasts. We buy into the emotion as significant or meaningful, and our attention is pulled toward things that perpetuate or exacerbate how we feel. If we can learn to instead direct our attention in a way that cuts off the fuel, emotions tend to dissipate more quickly. With practice, our experience with difficult emotions becomes more of a contained burn than an all-out forest fire.

Psychologists distinguish between two strategies for regulating emotions that we'll call *refocusing* and *reappraisal*.

Refocusing simply means directing your attention to something besides that which is fueling an emotion. When my family moved to Minnesota, one way I used this approach was by focusing on the opportunity to deepen my relationship with my sister rather than ruminating about the friendships from my childhood home that were growing weaker with time and distance. Refocusing is a perfectly reasonable and effective strategy as long as we don't use it to avoid parts of our life that require attention. By contrast, reappraisal involves changing the way that we evaluate our circumstances—perhaps recognizing that moving across the country is an opportunity to make new friends rather than simply a great injustice. Fundamentally, both refocusing and reappraisal rely on the two key skills of mindfulness. You make a choice to release one thing and to attend to another. So refocusing and reappraisal work hand in hand, allowing us to wield the skills of attending and releasing in order to have greater choice over what we experience and how we experience it.

Some people object that refocusing and reappraisal are somehow inauthentic—like rose-colored glasses that distort reality. These strategies may appear to prioritize how you feel over what's actually true, which seems like a disingenuous and ultimately doomed scheme. I have met and taught people who—out of fear of facing the reality of their life—have spun elaborate, self-serving, and ultimately counterproductive stories to avoid the truth. So I agree that these strategies can be misused. But I've also observed that it's easy for most people to avoid that trap, particularly if they are also committed to cultivating a willingness to experience emotion. That willingness removes the desperation to avoid difficult emotions, making it much less likely that someone will try to manage their emotions by ignoring the reality of their situation.

I'm a scientist not only by training but also by disposition, so the truth has always been my priority. In my search for truth, one thing I've learned is that many people mistake their opinions for facts. When we're frustrated with it being yet another rainy day, the objective truth is that it's raining. The truth of your frustration is only as stable as your negative evaluation, which is likely just your subjective opinion. I've personally found that mindfulness—and particularly decentering from thoughts—has allowed me to notice and release old ways of seeing the world that I thought were objective truth but that were actually subjective opinions.

For instance, it always seemed obvious to me that having a flight delayed was an inherently bad thing. Just as you would expect, most people's blood fills with cortisol the moment the delay is announced and they begin imagining all the ways that their careful plans will be interrupted. Yet there are often others who remain calm, trusting that they will manage the situation as best they can and that things will ultimately work out. It's not that one group sees the truth and the other doesn't. Both groups are keenly aware of the objective truth of the delay, but they diverge in powerful ways in their subjective opinions about that truth.

Of course, plenty of things in life are more demonstrably bad. It would be odd to respond to a diagnosis of terminal cancer by enthusiastically exclaiming, "Well, at least I wasn't hit by a truck this morning!" No one is recommending you lose touch with reality or pretend that things are great when they're not. But if you're like most people, you focus on things that upset you and evaluate your circumstances as problematic more than is necessary.

Attending and releasing are skills that take time to develop. Using these skills to work with challenging emotions is a fine art that develops progressively over years of practice. Yet I've had many students make rapid shifts in their emotional lives by earnestly applying these tools. Even if it does take some time, the benefits of using mindfulness to relate more skillfully to our emotions is well worth the effort. My personal experience over the last decade has been that difficult emotions are just not so difficult any more—not so heavy, intimidating, frequent, or long-lasting. Plus, mindfulness can help us cultivate positive emotions as well. That's what we'll discuss in the next chapter.

16 – CULTIVATING POSITIVE EMOTIONS

As we've discussed, mindfulness can transform our relationship to difficult emotions. This alone can transform our lives. Yet it's joy, gratitude, and love that can make life so sweet, and mindfulness is just as relevant to these emotions. A great deal of research shows that practicing mindfulness makes people happier. This can happen indirectly through the reduced stress, improved health, or strengthened relationships that can come from practicing mindfulness, but we can also use mindfulness to cultivate positive emotions more deliberately.

A piece of advice I often encounter is that you can't deliberately create happiness. According to this point of view, happiness is a byproduct of a life fully lived instead of something that can be pursued directly. My own experience has taught me countless times that although this advice is well-intentioned, it's ultimately misguided. To expect that a reliable happiness will spontaneously emerge without deliberate cultivation is simply unrealistic—something we'll discuss much more in later chapters. Fortunately, it's possible to purposefully cultivate happiness if you adopt the right strategy. As an experiment over the last few years, I've made a habit out of seeing whether in any given moment I can cultivate a little more joy. Of the thousands of times I've remembered to try, there was always a little more happiness available if I just placed my attention on the right thing. It's not always dramatic or enduring—sometimes it might be only a 10% improvement that lasts for a minute—but the opportunity is always there.

Everyone I know has something they could appreciate more than they do. We all take so much for granted. It's impossible not to. In our complex lives, how can we help but forget about all the things that are going well? The dilemma we all face is that no matter how much we do have, without gratitude we can still feel as though we don't have enough. From this perspective, I've come to realize that mindfulness provides us with the most obvious, most direct, and most effective way to cultivate happiness in our lives on a moment-by-moment basis. By taking charge of our focus as well as our evaluation of our circumstances, we can more consistently remember to appreciate the many things we do have. Mindfulness gives us the opportunity to deliberately appreciate this moment, one moment at a time.

Many people assume that positive emotions—just like negative emotions—are things that happen to us based mostly on external circumstances. Yet this perspective neglects the powerful role that we play in influencing our emotions. Because the emotions you feel are strongly influenced by where you focus, it's possible to use mindfulness to cultivate a whole variety of positive emotions. You just have to nurture the causes that give rise to a given emotion. Take love for example. Most people don't deliberately cultivate their love for their spouse, but why not? Sometimes I'll play music that reminds me of my wife and direct my mind to all the things I love about her. Soon enough, that loving feeling starts to become my predominant emotion. This is just one example of how changing the focus of our attention can shape our emotional experience.

As we'll discuss in later chapters, cultivating specific positive emotions can help prevent or resolve many of the most common obstacles people experience during meditation. For instance, cultivating kindness has a way of countering negativity. Although it takes practice and skill, generating positive emotion is a powerful tool for working with more negative emotions—we'll talk about this in detail in Part IV. When combined with a greater willingness to experience difficult emotions and more skill in dismantling counterproductive emotions, the deliberate cultivation of positive emotions gives us the choice to direct our emotional lives as we see fit.

Part III:

MEDITATION

17 - MEDITATION

Daily life provides countless opportunities to practice mindfulness, but your progress will be much faster if you also spend some time developing the skills of attending and releasing in meditation. Because these are such powerful skills, I have come to understand meditation as a crucially important part of living a deeply fulfilling and productive life. Yet meditation is not a quick or easy path. If it were quick and easy, then almost everyone would have walked it and the world would be filled with happy people. Meditation is a long and sometimes challenging journey. Fortunately, the path of meditation becomes easier and more beautiful the further you go.

Most of us start this journey in an overgrown forest dense with unskillful habits of thought, evaluation, and emotion. We often begin without understanding where meditation will take us, without a detailed map of how to get there, and without a strong commitment to going the distance. So it's no surprise that the vast majority never take more than a few steps along this path and never taste the freedom of where it leads.

Meditation is an acquired taste. No one sits down for the first time to watch their mind explode into bliss and transformative insight. Especially when you are first beginning to practice, meditation will sometimes feel difficult. It's not always easy to sit still or to look more closely at our often neglected minds. Yet as it goes with acquired tastes, meditation can become something you truly savor. It's a chance to unburden ourselves of the counterproductive habits of mind we lug around without even realizing it. It's a way to hone the skills of attending and releasing, as well as an opportunity to use these skills with ever greater precision to create a bright, joyful, and focused mind.

There are many different kinds of meditation, each with a somewhat different purpose. Yet all forms of meditation develop the skills of attending and releasing. Although you may want to focus your efforts on just one or two types of meditation, it's helpful to learn about several different kinds. In this book, we'll discuss three types: present moment awareness, mindful breathing, and open monitoring. If you understand the ways in which these meditations are similar to and different from one another, you will have a clear framework for interpreting other forms of meditation you encounter or want to try. In the following chapters, we'll discuss each of these types of meditation in turn.

Regardless of which specific kind of meditation you are practicing, there are a number of things to keep in mind. First, choose a suitable location. You certainly don't need total silence. As you know, your peripheral awareness will be filled with a constantly shifting variety of experiences, and you are not in conflict with any of them. On occasion, it's even useful to deliberately practice in highly distracting environments. But generally it's helpful to find a place where you won't be interrupted and where the level of distraction from your environment doesn't feel excessive.

Next, take a comfortable seated posture. The goal is to find a healthy posture that is comfortable and that will help you stay alert. You can meditate lying down, but you will be enormously more susceptible to drowsiness (more on this later). So unless a physical limitation prevents you, sit upright on a cushion or a chair. Your hands can rest in your lap or on your knees, with your elbows tucked gently into your sides. I like to think about my head gently floating to create a long supported spine. You may close your eyes if you wish as long as you don't get drowsy. Otherwise, just lower your gaze to a comfortable space in front of you. These simple guidelines are a good place to start, but posture is a hard thing to teach effectively through text. Check out the video we posted at this book's website at *http://empiricalwisdom.com/books.*

Third, clearly instruct your mind as to what you want it to do. Everyone has multiple goals to juggle, which leads many people to launch into a meditation session half-heartedly. They want to meditate, but they also have other things on their mind they would like to entertain. Then they spend half the time on the cushion thinking about those other things without any genuine effort to stay present. It's important to approach each session by dedicating yourself fully to the practice. To make sure that your mind knows what to do, I recommend that you begin by saying to yourself two or three times something like "Now is the time to pay attention to the sensations of my breath and to let everything else go."

Fourth, give yourself a little nudge toward enjoying meditation. Over time, this will happen naturally. But particularly at the beginning, sitting still and trying to focus your mind can feel a bit challenging or tedious. You don't have to pretend you're having a great time when you're not, but be open to enjoying the process. More on this later, too.

Finally, end your practice by taking a moment to savor the experience and give yourself a little credit for having done it. Then reflect on how it went. Meditation is a craft. Each time you practice, your skill improves. You can accelerate your learning curve by taking a little time to reflect on each session. What went well? Were there any distractions that kept coming up again and again? Which of the obstacles to meditation—something we'll discuss in detail in later chapters—were most disruptive? In the long-term, you will make much faster progress if you jot down a few notes after you sit, especially if you make a habit of reviewing them before your next session.

People often ask *how* to gauge their progress in meditation. From month to month, you can expect to see improvements in the stability of your attention. If you don't, you should pause to identify and troubleshoot whatever is stalling your progress. For many, it's simply an inconsistency in practice. But it's also common that there is an obstacle to deepening meditation that isn't being identified or addressed, which we'll begin exploring in Part IV.

Yet from day to day—and even week to week—the level of your concentration isn't the best way to gauge progress. In fact, it's more likely to lead to false discouragement than anything else. Many internal and external factors influence how distracted your mind is on any given day. Some days you will be distracted even if you are applying all the right strategies. To conclude that you're not making progress would be mistaken. The more skillful criteria to gauge your progress over the short-term is whether you're practicing with a genuine commitment to give it your best and learn as much as you can. If you do this consistently, you can be sure that your skill will improve over time.

Keeping these points in mind, we'll take the next few chapters to go into detail about how to practice three different kinds of meditation. The first type we'll discuss is present moment awareness.

18 – PRESENT MOMENT AWARENESS MEDITATION

Everything you've learned in the earlier chapters is about to pay off in a big way as we start down the path of meditation. The first part of this path is one of my very favorites—present moment awareness. As you may recall from chapter three, present moment awareness involves anchoring your attention on whatever is happening right now and releasing any thoughts about the past or future. You can practice present moment awareness as you go about your day, but you can also practice it in formal meditation. I recommend sitting in the same posture for this kind of meditation as you would for any other. Then clearly instruct your mind that it's time to pay attention to things happening in the present moment. You might like to start by first listening to all the sounds in your environment or by tuning into the sensations in your body. Then you can let your attention wander anywhere it likes as long as you don't get caught up in thoughts about the past or future.

Most meditation teachers begin by introducing mindful breathing, but I prefer to start with present moment awareness.

It's not better or worse—or even easier or harder. And you should practice both. But many people learn and practice mindful breathing to the exclusion of present moment awareness, which is a mistake for several reasons.

First, starting with present moment awareness helps us keep in mind from the beginning that mindfulness is not about shutting out the world. The present moment is such a broad anchor, so we get to invite all the richness and diversity of experience into our practice.

Second, present moment awareness translates very naturally into the rest of our lives. It is rarely appropriate during daily life to focus on the sensations of our breath to the exclusion of everything else, but during much of the day it is perfectly functional and even beneficial to be focused on the present moment. This helps us appreciate how our meditation practice is relevant to the rest of our lives.

Third, present moment awareness forces us to get clear about what it means to have a broad anchor. It requires that we approach meditation with an investigative mind. We have to figure out through our own direct experience what it means to be mindful even as our attention alternates from one thing to the next. This can be a little confusing initially—it's a bit more straight forward to know whether you're on track when you use a narrow anchor like the breath. But it's better to face and clarify this confusion early on so that you truly understand how mindfulness works.

Sometimes this confusion shows up as feeling scattered as your mind jumps endlessly from one sensation to the next. Although it can feel odd to watch your mind do this, it's an informative exercise to observe how frantic your attention can be. Keep in mind that when practicing present moment awareness, you can always anchor your attention on something more specific—a sight, sound, or even the sensations of your breath. You just don't have to stay there. Whenever you like— or whenever your mind decides on its own—you can shift to something else happening in the present moment and focus there instead.

Since there's so much to pay attention to, many people expect that staying in the present moment will be easy. It's usually not. Most of us have a strong tendency to think about the past and future much more than is helpful. Even during the activities in which it is generally easiest to be absorbed—like a delicious meal—there's a surprising tendency for the mind to leave the present moment. In fact, newcomers to mindfulness are sometimes shocked to discover just how hard it is to stay anchored in the present. At times, it can seem impossible.

It's normal to feel a little discouraged or frustrated when you find your mind inadvertently racing to the past or future despite your best intentions. When this happens, it's important to remember that these thoughts are not problems—they are opportunities to practice the skills of attending and releasing.

I also find it useful to consider that no matter how many times we get distracted, the nature of reality is conspiring to always bring us back to this moment. It's like a bird on a ship in the middle of the ocean—no matter how far it flies away, it has to eventually come back to the ship because there's nowhere else to land. No matter how far our minds may drift, we must inevitably come back to the present moment. This moment is where everything takes place. No one has ever done anything in the future. Everything that has ever been accomplished was done in the present moment. This means that every single time you start elaborating a thought about the past or future, reality will eventually bring you back to the here and now.

In fact, it may have occurred to you that even our thoughts of the past and future arise now, in this constantly unfolding present. We slip into thinking about the past or future without ever actually leaving the present. But thinking about the past or future does distract us from everything else that's happening right now. Sometimes that can be worth it. After all, it's important to remember our past and plan our future, and it can be enjoyable to reminisce or daydream. The goal should be to do these things to the degree that they benefit us. Yet most of us have a strong tendency to think about the past and future much more than is helpful. We replay tough memories over and over for no reason. We worry about things that never even happen. We go through life weighed down by unproductive thoughts of the past and future, often without realizing how much lighter we would feel if we simply decided to set down these burdens. Airlines set weight limits for your luggage because they don't want all your baggage to weigh them down. Birds don't carry suitcases. No one is forcing us to spend our lives dragging around stressful thoughts about the past and the future. We can choose to come back to the lightness of present moment awareness anytime.

You might ask, what's so great about being in the present moment? Isn't this where all the trials of life show up? Pain, loss, sadness—aren't those always happening in the now? Of course, you would be right. There is a wonderful lightness to present moment awareness, but it's not because mindfulness turns the present into a fairy tale. Being present to the hard things is no cake walk. Yet keep in mind that a huge proportion of our suffering is spun by our thinking minds— the thoughts and evaluations that make us struggle over the struggle. Not to mention the thoughts that create struggle out of thin air. So the lightness comes from learning to be in the present moment without a looming inner narrative ruminating over the past, worrying about the future, and generally making things worse. Then yes, sometimes the present moment is still difficult. But often it's like slipping into a warm bath.

Over time, you'll start to notice that even thoughts that seem to be about the present are often thoughts about what happened just a moment ago. As soon as you begin elaborating on one experience, you lose touch with the ever changing present. With practice, you can start to release even those thoughts that seem to be about what's happening right now. When you release all thoughts as they arise, your awareness of everything else that's happening right now becomes even more heightened. It's as though you're greeting one experience immediately after the next without getting pulled out of the moment and into your head. Just be careful not to make thoughts the enemy. They'll always keep showing up, giving you lots of opportunities to practice.

The enjoyment that I now experience from present moment awareness is worth a thousand fold the investment of time it has taken to develop the skills of attending and releasing. In order to be able to reliably access this state of mind, it's important to spend some time practicing it during formal meditation where it can be your sole priority. Over time, you'll be able to access a similar state even as you are taking a walk or relaxing at home. If you like, present moment awareness can even become your default state whenever there isn't some more meaningful way to engage your mind. In this way, daily mindfulness practice and formal meditation can reinforce one another as you accelerate toward ever greater levels of presence of mind.

19 – MINDFUL BREATHING MEDITATION

Life is short, and the suggestion to spend any significant amount of it focusing on the breath can be a hard sell. At any moment, there may be dozens of other ways to use our time that may at first seem more productive or enjoyable. After all, it's easy to overlook just how powerfully the skills of attending and releasing can improve our lives. And without practice, it's impossible to know how nice it feels to simply rest with the breath. This creates a reluctance that stops many people who take an interest in meditation from ever developing true mastery of it. But if you are willing to practice mindful breathing consistently in order to discover for yourself what's possible, you may be surprised at how much you come to enjoy it.

Mindful breathing is far and away the most widely practiced form of meditation—and for good reason. The breath is an excellent anchor for cultivating mindfulness. It's always present, allowing us to practice whenever we wish. The sensations of breathing are dynamic, which makes it easier to pay attention to than something like a rock. But it's not inherently captivating like a great film, so it challenges your ability to stay focused. The breath is also an automatic process over which we can exert deliberate conscious control, giving us the opportunity to purposefully change the way we breathe but also the opportunity to practice letting go of control completely. Finally, focusing on the breath becomes a highly pleasant experience over time. This helps reinforce our practice and eventually serves as a natural bridge to the absorption states of advanced meditation.

As you know, practicing mindfulness generally requires that you choose an anchor (though we'll talk about one exception to this in the next chapter). During mindful breathing, your anchor will be the sensations of breathing. How can you tell whether you are breathing in or out? Whatever sensations of breathing you feel most strongly, make those your anchor. This may be the rising and falling of your chest and belly, or perhaps just the sensation of air passing in and out below your nose.

At times, it's useful to deliberately control the rhythm of your breath. If you feel anxious, you can breathe slow and deep to relax. If you're sleepy, breathing rapidly can build more energy. It's also worthwhile to search for a way of breathing that's particularly comfortable, which will make it easier to stay present. Yet eventually you will want to release any control over the breath and let it find a natural rhythm. This isn't always easy to do. Simply watching the breath can sometimes lead us to inadvertently control it, which for some people can make the breath feel uncomfortable. Rest assured that with just a little time and by redirecting your attention to the sensations rather than the pace of your breath, your body will naturally smooth everything out.

Remember, you will inevitably become distracted from your breath. How you react to this distraction is at the heart of meditation. First of all, relax. There's a subtle tendency for the mind to respond to distraction with frustration and tension, which is not the state of mind you're trying to cultivate. Until you automatically respond to distraction without tension, take a brief moment to deliberately relax as you refocus your attention to your breath. Remember, even if you get distracted hundreds of times in a meditation, you can still benefit from the session. The distraction is the opportunity to release.

Because mindfulness sometimes involves releasing thoughts rather than elaborating them into extended trains of thought, the thinking mind is often viewed as being at odds with meditation. Yet there are ways of using the thinking mind to deepen your practice. For example, when you set your intention to practice at the beginning of a meditation, you use thoughts to clearly instruct your mind on what you want it do.

Another helpful way to involve the thinking mind is to count your breath. Part of the reason this is effective is that it occupies your inner voice in a strategic way, making it less available to distracting trains of thoughts. There's no one right way to do it, but I like to count every exhalation so that every complete breath counts as one. Try counting ten breaths and then starting over. If you lose track, just start again at one. The goal isn't to become a professional breath counter, but to use this tool to stabilize the mind.

Alternatively, you could simply choose to repeat a word using your inner voice on each inhalation and exhalation. For years, I've fallen asleep at night paying attention to my breath. If my mind is particularly active on a given night, I'll often say "relax" as I breathe in and "restore" as I breathe out. I repeat this over and over, which occupies my thinking mind so it doesn't get swept up in extended trains of thought. This approach works equally well during formal meditation.

Another common strategy for involving the thinking mind is to tag anything that distracts you with a brief label—like hearing, seeing, tasting, smelling, feeling, or thinking. Some people swear by this strategy, so you should try it out. It certainly helps keep your thinking mind in the game. Yet as you become more experienced in meditation, you may find that distracting thoughts and perceptions come and go so quickly that trying to label them all can turn into a bizarre and endless inner chant. A good rule of thumb is that if assigning a label takes more of your attention than the distraction did, the label isn't necessary.

It's important to remember that the goal of involving the thinking mind is to help you stay with the breath, not to distract you from it. Counting your breath does distract you a little bit from the physical sensations of breathing, but it's worth it because you end up spending much less time in extended states of obliviousness to your anchor. Count the breath, but place more of your attention on the sensations themselves. Then once you can count the breath for several minutes without major distractions, let the thinking mind fall away completely and redirect the attention it was using to the sensations of breathing.

20 – OPEN-MONITORING MEDITATION

Open-monitoring meditation has been traditionally practiced only after developing expertise with meditations that cultivate focused attention, like present moment awareness and mindful breathing. It's not that open-monitoring is a superior type of meditation, but it is more nuanced and advanced. Yet these days, many teachers introduce open-monitoring much earlier. In fact, for some people it is their *first* introduction to meditation. For others, it is taught alongside or even jumbled up with other forms of meditation without clear distinction about how it is similar or different. Not surprisingly, open-monitoring is often misunderstood.

Unlike present moment awareness or mindful breathing, open-monitoring is unique in that you don't try to narrow your focus in any way. For this reason, it's sometimes called *open attention* or *choiceless awareness*. Occasionally, it's also called *mindfulness meditation*, but this term means different things to different people. In my view, it also mistakenly suggests that mindfulness is somehow less relevant to other forms of meditation.

The key distinguishing feature of open-monitoring is that you practice releasing without having an anchor to attend to. This can be tricky. Attending is a natural and spontaneous process that happens all the time. So what happens when you don't have any particular place to focus and yet you constantly release your attention from anywhere it gets captured?

In both open-monitoring and present moment awareness, your attention will jump around from one thing to the next. The key difference is that in present moment awareness, you can attend as much as you like. You can focus on sounds for a minute, then watch your breath for a few seconds, and then shift your attention to what you see around you. In present moment awareness, you can switch your focus from one thing to another or even to hold it one place, as long as you're not elaborating thoughts about the past or future.

In open-monitoring, you choose to forego deliberately attending to any specific anchor. Of course, your mind will still automatically attend to things. That's what the mind naturally does, and you're not trying to stop it just like you wouldn't try to stop thoughts from arising. Whenever you notice that you're attending to something, you simply release it. This generally leads your attention to fluctuate even more rapidly than during present moment awareness. Because you're noticing so many different things for brief periods of time, open-monitoring can give you the sense that you are highly aware of everything happening in the moment. Yet that broad awareness is not the goal. If you make it the goal, your mind will have a hard time resisting the impulse to deliberately shift your attention around from one thing to the next. The goal is to simply practice releasing without having an anchor to attend to. A broad awareness is one possible and natural consequence.

Because you don't have an anchor, the four stage

continuum of focused attention—absorbed, focused, distracted, oblivious—doesn't apply here. In fact, you can't really be distracted during open-monitoring because there's no anchor to get distracted from. But when something captures your attention, you might forget to release it. So the challenge is to continuously release whatever grabs your attention.

By now you know how important it is to respond to distraction as an opportunity rather than a problem. In open-monitoring, the same logic applies to attending. You cannot stop your mind from attending, so don't start open-monitoring meditation with the wild expectation that your mind will enter some unmoving yet all-knowing state of transcendence. It's more likely that your mind will flit around like a coked up hummingbird on the first day of spring. Your job is to make sure that as soon as you taste one flower, you release any inclination to stay with it so that your mind can flit over to the next.

Of course, perceptions will often stay in your conscious awareness for more than a split second. Sometimes that is because your mind is directing attention to that thing, but other times it's simply because that thing is a strong enough signal to force itself through the filter of attention. If a plane flies by overhead, the rumbling sound of its engines may fluctuate between the spotlight of attention and peripheral awareness for the entire thirty seconds that it takes to pass by. You are not in conflict with the sound. Sometimes you won't even be able to tell whether you're aware of it because you're attending to it or because it's just a salient part of your environment. With time and lots of practice, that distinction will become more clear. Regardless, you can always return to the intention to release.

It's worth circling back to what *releasing* means because, as we've discussed, it's subtle. I like to think about it as interrupting the mind's natural tendency to engage. We engage with thoughts by elaborating them and we engage with perceptions of our environment by continuing to give them more attention. Releasing disrupts this process. I suspect that the brain achieves this through a process known as inhibition—the ability to interrupt an automatic or habitual way of attending. Usually this is followed immediately by focusing our attention somewhere else, but the premise of open-monitoring is that releasing and attending can be separated. Empirical research also suggests that these processes are distinct. But that distinction is not always easy to observe in our own experience. Practicing open-monitoring is a uniquely effective way to train your mind's ability to simply release, though it does take considerable practice.

One common mistake that prevents some people from distinguishing between attending and releasing is inadvertently letting an anchor slip in the back door. At first, it's hard to even conceive of what it means to release without an anchor. So without realizing that they're just creating a new anchor, they start redirecting attention to a perceptual blackness, a conceptual sense of emptiness, or a word like "release" or "open". If you're deliberately directing your attention somewhere again and again, that's an anchor! People come up with extraordinarily creative ways to reintroduce an anchor, so be on the look-out.

Another common challenge in open-monitoring is feeling like there's no place to rest. If there's no anchor to return to, where is your mind allowed to go? Some people feel a sense of pressure in trying to release everything as soon as they attend to it. It's helpful to remember the difference between releasing and suppressing thoughts. Trying to suppress thoughts only backfires and creates tension. So you don't suppress thoughts, you just release them when they arise. Similarly, you're not trying to shut anything out during open-monitoring. Instead, I like to think about constantly relaxing the impulse to engage. Moment after moment, you just keep releasing. So rather than finding a *place* to rest, you just rest in letting go.

Open-monitoring is an advanced practice, so don't be discouraged if it doesn't make perfect sense to you after reading a chapter about it. There's no rush to make open-monitoring a part of your meditation practice, though you also don't have to wait until you're an expert to try it. I like to teach open-monitoring early on to give students a more complete understanding of mindfulness and to prepare them for when they inevitably encounter it elsewhere. I also encourage those with roughly a hundred hours of meditation experience to give it their best shot. It can force you to figure out through your own experience some subtleties about how the skills of attending and releasing work. Nevertheless, my advice would be to dedicate most of your time to present moment awareness and mindful breathing until those practices are strong. Then when you return to open-monitoring, your solid foundation will allow you to pursue this style of meditation to new heights.

21 - INTROSPECTION

To make progress at any type of meditation, you need to monitor what's happening in your mind. This requires *introspection*: the observation of one's own mental state. There are two kinds of introspection. You can simply direct your attention to what's happening in your mind, which produces a kind of *experiential* introspection. You can also use the thinking mind to reflect on what you're experiencing, which is something we'll call *conceptual introspection*.

To illustrate how these two kinds of introspection are related, consider what you would do if I asked you whether you felt hungry. To answer this question, you have to direct the spotlight of attention inward. First, your attention is directed to how you feel, perhaps seeking any familiar sensations of hunger in your stomach. Then in order to answer the question, you put that experience into words. The first step of directing attention inward creates an experiential awareness of what's happening in your body, regardless of whether you give that experience a label. The optional second step of putting the experience into words produces a conceptual form of introspection. Both experiential and conceptual awareness can be helpful during meditation, and both require some attention. We'll return to this distinction in a minute.

When introspection is absent, we can get derailed by distractions without realizing what's happening. Everyone has had this experience while reading—your eyes are still skimming the page but your mind starts musing about something completely unrelated. If you had introspective awareness of what you were doing, you would either stop pointlessly scanning the page or you would stop mind-wandering. But you're not really aware of what's happening in your mind, so you keep doing both. Then suddenly it dawns on you that you were mind-wandering, and that introspective awareness provides the opportunity to refocus.

It's hard to make it very far in meditation without cultivating a moment-by-moment awareness of what's happening in your mind. In particular, you need to have introspective awareness of where you are directing the spotlight of attention. You can't introspect about *everything*—your physical sensations, focus, thoughts, evaluations, moods, personality, hang ups—all at once. Instead, the highest priority during meditation is staying aware of where the spotlight of attention is focused. Eventually you want to get to a place where you notice distractions almost as soon as they arise so that you can quickly release them. This requires an almost continuous introspective awareness. You have to notice your mind getting distracted *as it's happening* so that you can course-correct right away. In this way, introspection works a bit like those rumble strips along highways that make a loud noise if you start to veer off the road. They help you notice as soon as you get off course.

In any moment, you can develop introspective awareness

by directing the spotlight of attention inward to observe the state of your mind. Remember that the spotlight can only be focused on one thing at a time. This means you can't use the spotlight for introspective awareness while at the same time focusing the spotlight on your anchor. When the spotlight is occupied by introspective awareness, one of two things will happen to your anchor: it will either stay in peripheral awareness (meaning you are *distracted* from your anchor) or you will stop being aware of it altogether (meaning you are *oblivious* to it). That makes meditation a kind of balancing act. You need to redirect the spotlight inward in order to cultivate introspective awareness, but not so much that you become oblivious to your anchor.

Fortunately, introspection can also exist in peripheral awareness. When the spotlight returns to your anchor after an introspective check-in, you often maintain some introspection through your peripheral awareness. This means that with practice, it's possible to have the spotlight jump back and forth between your anchor and introspection in a way that keeps both things in awareness most of the time. When the spotlight is focused on your anchor, introspection is in peripheral awareness. When the spotlight is on introspection, your anchor is in peripheral awareness. As the spotlight jumps back and forth, you alternate between being *focused* on your anchor and being *distracted* from it, but you're rarely *oblivious* to it. It might sound strange to intentionally distract yourself from your anchor, but it's worth it in this case. Those temporary distractions allow you to sustain a continuous introspective awareness that makes it less likely that you will lose track of your anchor altogether.

We can consciously direct the spotlight of attention, and we do it all the time. Indirectly, we can also consciously influence what is in peripheral awareness. As I just mentioned, one way to do this is with the spotlight: peripheral awareness is more likely to include whatever has been in the spotlight of attention most recently. A second way to influence what makes it into peripheral awareness is through our values and priorities. Lots of unconscious mental processes shape how attention operates, thereby governing what makes it into conscious awareness. These processes are influenced by what we value. As an example, consider what happens when someone is in the market for a new car. Because of this new priority, they start noticing brands of cars on the road that they otherwise would have completely ignored. The same principle can be applied to introspective awareness. If you make introspection a high priority, many unconscious mental processes will help introspective awareness occur more often in both the spotlight of attention and peripheral awareness.

To make this concrete, how specifically should you cultivate introspective awareness during meditation? First, remind yourself that this is a crucially important aspect of meditation. When you start a session, recall the importance of staying aware of what's happening in your mind. This will help recruit all those unconscious mental processes to start working in support of introspective awareness.

Next, alternate the spotlight of attention back and forth between your anchor and introspection. One way to do this is to simply try to stay aware of both. That will automatically lead your spotlight to jump back and forth between the two. I give more emphasis to my anchor than my introspection, but you can experiment and find a balance that works for you.

A specific strategy I have found particularly effective during meditation is to periodically ask myself "Am I present?" or "Where is my focus?" without consciously answering the question. Asking a question without answering it automatically sends your mind in search of an answer. For instance, I might count three exhalations and then on the fourth use my inner voice to ask whether I'm present. This strategy invites such frequent introspection that your awareness of what's going on in your mind can feel almost continuous even though you never lose track of your breath.

Introspective awareness is essential for meditation, and it's also useful when you're practicing mindfulness in daily life. In both contexts, it helps you notice when your attention starts to drift away from your anchor. While driving, for example, introspection can help you notice when you start getting too engrossed in a train of thought that is distracting you from the road. Yet there are some activities where a deliberate effort to cultivate introspective awareness is neither necessary nor helpful. Good examples for me include reading scientific papers and writing. I can often get quite absorbed in these activities, losing myself completely in them with only occasional distraction. Personally, trying to maintain continuous introspective awareness during these activities can be more distracting than helpful. Focusing even a little bit of my attention on monitoring my experience can make it harder to be fully immersed in the experience itself, which is often what is necessary for me to write well or read a complex paper. From this vantage point, introspective awareness is a crucially important way of correcting course when we get distracted, but it's not *always* needed. Sometimes it's fine to just let yourself get absorbed in something—a great book, film, or conversation—without trying to maintain introspective awareness. It's like air conditioning that you might leave running most of the time, but it's also okay to turn it off.

22 - EFFORT

The amount of effort you invest during meditation has a big effect on how quickly you will make progress. However, there is such wildly discrepant advice circulating about the role of effort in meditation that it's hard to know how much effort we should actually exert while practicing. At one extreme, many teachers say that meditation requires that we let go of effort. They suggest that meditating is like falling asleep—*trying* to do it just gets in the way. This perspective claims that a better approach is to just relax and observe as the mind calms down on its own. Many find this advice helpful, and it can assist with letting go of the tension from our daily lives as well as the part of us that chronically wants to make things different from how they are. But making no effort also leads some people to float aimlessly through their practice, spending a lot of time completely lost in thought and barely progressing.

At the other extreme, some suggest we make a profound and continuous effort. This perspective generally assumes that greater effort tends to lead to better outcomes in meditation. Some ancient teachings even suggest that life is so short and the benefits of actively cultivating our minds are so great that we should practice with the same sense of urgency as we would respond to being on fire. Some find that this advice brings a whole new level of motivation and resourcefulness to their practice, but it can feel stressful and too extreme to others. When I was first getting serious about meditation, I remember telling friends about how unwavering my focus became when I imagined my life depended on not losing track of my breath. Some of them understandably thought I was being a little too intense.

Of course, one obvious alternative is a compromise between these extremes. We can aim for middle ground, finding the Goldilocks zone of meditative effort—not too much, not too little, but just right. Like an instrument that is tuned to just the right pitch, we can tune our effort to the optimal level. But what is this optimal level? And is there no more nuance to this equation than just a compromise between trying too hard and trying too little?

Before we decide how much effort to invest, we should first reflect on what *effort* actually is. Effort is commonly defined as the expenditure of energy or as strenuous work, which mistakenly suggests that effort is something that (1) utilizes a limited resource and (2) involves some physical or mental strain. These two assumptions about effort are widespread, but we should be wary of them because they have serious implications for our chances at engaging optimally with effort during meditation.

The way we think about effort in general is strongly influenced by how we experience *physical* effort in particular. Exercise challenges our muscles, heart, and lungs in a way that conforms to widespread assumptions about effort. First, it draws from a limited resource because we can only exercise for so long. Second, it involves some strain because exercise can be physically uncomfortable. As the demands we place on our bodies approach our actual physiological capacities, the subjective sense of strain grows stronger. This is a good thing because it stops us from pushing our bodies to the point of exhaustion and injury. It's also true that regularly challenging our bodies makes them stronger, but we never escape the reality that exercise taxes limited physiological capacities and that greater demands are associated with greater physical discomfort. This is likely why people tend to choose the easier of two physical tasks when given the option—something that scientists call *effort avoidance*.

Being strategic about physical effort in order to conserve energy and protect the body from injury makes logical sense, but research shows that we avoid mental effort too. Given the chance to solve easier or harder problems, people tend to choose the easy ones. Some highly popularized research also initially showed that engaging in one challenging mental task led to worse performance on a subsequent task. A common interpretation of these findings has been that—like physical effort—mental effort draws from a limited resource. However, more recent research has demonstrated that our beliefs about effort determine whether we are depleted by demanding mental tasks. It is the *belief* that mental effort is a limited resource that makes us susceptible to feeling drained after using mental effort. By contrast, people who believe that mental energy is not depleted by its use can generally maintain high performance even after completing a challenging mental task.

This line of reasoning suggests a profound possibility—that there is a kind of mental effort which is inexhaustible. In the context of mindfulness, this corresponds to the ability to attend without strain to your anchor and to release distractions as they arise. My experience suggests that this effort can be sustained continuously without growing weaker. Certainly the neurons that allow you to attend and release are drawing oxygen and glucose from your bloodstream, but so does your always beating heart and your always breathing lungs.

You may already have an experience in your life that illustrates this kind of inexhaustible effort. Can you think of something that you find so enjoyable and engaging that you could do it for a long time without it making you tired? Many people can read chapter after chapter in a great novel without it exhausting them even though they are constantly focusing their attention, interpreting thousands of sentences, and keeping track of a complex story. Their mind is highly active and extremely focused, but they're not depleted by it. With practice, meditation can be the same way. In fact, it's possible to sit for an hour—constantly trying to attend to your anchor while releasing distractions—and to finish feeling completely refreshed.

To connect with this inexhaustible effort, we have to learn to dissociate it from the unnecessary and unskillful tension that often gets layered on top. Let's call this *effort baggage*. Without even realizing it, we often hold physical tension in our bodies and create mental tension through habitual patterns of unskillful thinking and evaluation. As we sit in meditation, we might get frustrated with our progress, resent the pain in our back, and tense our brow as we try to focus. It's not uncommon to feel like these things are part of the effort we're making, but often they are just tension and stress that we associate with actual effort. This effort baggage can fatigue us much more than attending to the breath and releasing distraction.

It's helpful to view mindfulness as something that *provides* energy rather than something that *consumes* it. In principle, we could be mindful all day without growing tired. I like to think of mindfulness as a form of awakened rest. To achieve this, we have to become aware of the tension and stress that we misconstrue as effort. Meditation provides a great context to explore this. Where is there tension in your body? If it's unnecessary, can you let it go? Where is there stress in your mind? If it's unnecessary, can you let it go? When you've released the stress and tension and you're still guiding your mind to stay with the breath, you've connected with inexhaustible effort. Now you can exert a profound and continuous effort during your practice—attending and releasing on a moment-by-moment basis—without layering on the effort baggage that would exhaust you. As a result, the harder you try, the more rested you'll feel.

Part IV:

THE OBSTACLES

23 – THE INEVITABLE OBSTACLES

By now, you know a great deal about mindfulness. You understand that attending and releasing are fundamental skills that allow you to have greater choice over what you experience and how you experience it. You've learned strategies for using these skills to guide your thoughts, evaluations, and emotions in ways that can improve your life. You also know how to cultivate these skills in different types of meditation, including present moment awareness, mindful breathing, and open-monitoring. A surprisingly small proportion of the people I've met who have been exposed to mindfulness or meditation have developed this level of understanding. Yet if this were the extent of your learning, you would still be woefully unprepared for the inevitable challenges you'll face in meditation.

Let's imagine you're one of the lucky ones who takes to meditation right away. Your first experiences with it are positive, and maybe you even notice your concentration improving week by week. Then just as your enthusiasm for mindfulness reaches an all-time high, you plateau. Your progress seems to slow down or even stop altogether. Your interest in meditating declines and it starts to feel like a chore. You find it impossible to stay with your anchor for any length of time, and you start to wonder if you're really getting anything out of it. Part of you just wants to get each meditation over with almost as soon as it begins. What happened? Where did things go wrong?

There are certain obstacles to developing mindfulness that are universal. Everyone experiences these challenges at some point, and they can easily derail your progress and diminish your motivation to practice meditation. It is crucially important to learn what these obstacles are and how to handle them, yet the vast majority of people I meet who practice meditation have never been adequately trained in how to deal with the obstacles that they will inevitably encounter. If you don't learn how to address these obstacles, your progress will be slow and you will only be able to go so far. Additionally, learning about these obstacles can help you realize that the challenges and resistance you will likely experience while practicing mindfulness are not unique to you. Rather than feel frustrated or interpret the challenges as personal failings, you can instead apply effective strategies that allow you to take your practice to the next level.

Over thousands of years, contemplative traditions have developed helpful descriptions of the most common obstacles to meditation. These obstacles are barriers to deepening your meditation practice. Each obstacle will inevitably show up in your practice at some point, and they are also highly relevant to the quality of your mindfulness during daily life. We'll review six obstacles in total: drowsiness, discomfort, doubt, ill-will, restlessness, and sensory desire. Because these obstacles are so important, we will spend a chapter on each of them.

Although each obstacle requires a somewhat unique

solution, there is a general approach you can take to working with the obstacles that I strongly recommend. The process includes five steps: (1) understand the obstacle, (2) recognize the obstacle when it arises in your experience, (3) avoid letting the obstacle convince you that it is helpful, (4) release the obstacle, and (5) if the obstacle persists, either apply a remedy or cultivate the opposing quality.

Step One: Understand the obstacle

You have to know what you're up against. Otherwise you could encounter an obstacle over and over without understanding what's happening. You might feel like you're making no progress, but you don't realize it's because one of the obstacles to meditation is getting in your way. So the first step is to get clear on what the obstacles are and how they tend to show up for people. We'll do that together in the next six chapters.

Step Two: Recognize the obstacle when it arises in your experience

You're not immune to these obstacles. You will experience them. There's no way around that. In fact, one or more will be present in almost every single meditation you ever complete. Yet many people don't realize when these obstacles are present even as they are hitting right up against them. You can only take action to counter the obstacles that you notice. This is yet another reason why introspective awareness is so crucial to meditation.

Step Three: Avoid letting the obstacle convince you that it is good for you

These obstacles are like the mythic sirens whose

enchanting singing would lure deluded sailors to crash into the rocky coastline of an island. The enchanting voices seemed like a great thing even as they led the sailors to their demise. The obstacles to meditation do something similar. A hint of drowsiness comes with the enchanting message that we should let ourselves sink into our sleepiness, so we close our eyes and become even more drowsy. The obstacles convince us that they are valid and even helpful, so we follow them until our meditation crashes into distraction, frustration, and stalled progress. In the following chapters, you'll develop an understanding of each of the obstacles that will make it easier for you to see through them when they arise during meditation.

Step Four: Release the obstacle

Before you do anything more complicated to overcome an obstacle that has shown up during your meditation, first try to simply release it. Remember that thoughts, evaluations, and emotions generally have power over us to the degree that we engage with them. If we find ourselves thinking, "I'm awful at this and I don't know if I'll ever get good at meditation", sometimes simply letting that thought come and go is enough. Then just get right back to attending to your chosen anchor. Even if the obstacle comes back, we can always release it again. As long as we avoid giving more energy to the obstacle by entertaining it, we're taking a big step toward limiting its influence over us.

Step Five: If the obstacle persists, apply a strategy to counter it

Releasing the obstacle when it arises isn't always enough. Even if you release the impulse to close your eyes when you get drowsy, you may still feel tired throughout the rest of your meditation. So if an obstacle is stubborn or starts to meaningfully influence the quality of your practice, it's time to be more proactive. Each obstacle has specific remedies—like opening your eyes and raising your gaze to counter drowsiness—that will help you address the obstacle in a more substantial way. Each obstacle also has what we'll call an opposing quality—something positive you can cultivate that is an opposing force and natural solution for a given obstacle. For instance, the opposing quality for restlessness is appreciation. If you take a moment to appreciate something enjoyable or meaningful about what is happening right here and now, your mind will be much less inclined to want to rush off to somewhere else. We'll discuss both effective remedies and the opposing qualities for all six obstacles in the following chapters.

Meditating without overcoming the obstacles is like running with heavy ankle weights, only rather than making you stronger it gives you bad knees. Don't do it. There are truly effective strategies for countering all the obstacles, and you will learn them in the next six chapters. We'll discuss the obstacles primarily in the context of meditation, but you should keep in mind that they are also present during daily life. The strategies for working with the obstacles during meditation usually work in daily life as well. If you get good at countering the obstacles in one context, you will have no trouble overcoming them in the other.

24 - DROWSINESS

The first obstacle that many people face when beginning to practice meditation is drowsiness. When introducing mindfulness into college and high school classrooms, it's common for three quarters of a class to experience drowsiness during a meditation that lasts only a few minutes. It's a little crazy that so many people are going through their lives this sleep-deprived, but it's the reality in countless classrooms, boardrooms, and living rooms around the world.

Mindfulness practice can be an opportunity to recognize that our bodies and minds need more sleep. Meditation removes a lot of stimulation—both external sources (like music, videos, and interactions with other people) and internal ones (like planning, analyzing, or daydreaming). As soon as this stimulation subsides, a sleep-deprived mind instantly tries to seize the opportunity to catch up on the rest it desperately needs. Most people who are sleep deprived keep themselves alert throughout the day using a potent blend of caffeine and stimulation. If you take either component away, they start to drag. People often realize how important caffeine is to their alertness, but many fail to recognize just how much the stimulation element is sustaining them. Meditation will help make this very clear.

Meditating without enough sleep is an uphill battle the whole way. I've been there myself countless times. If you can't stay alert during meditation, your progress will be slow. Even if you manage to stay focused on your anchor, the acuity of your awareness will inevitably drop. Drowsiness also makes it harder to sustain introspection, which means you'll be less likely to catch yourself when you do start to drift off course.

Our level of drowsiness during meditation can serve as a good test for whether we are getting enough rest, and the very best solution to drowsiness is getting consistent high quality sleep. Research shows that most people underestimate the amount of sleep they need and overestimate the amount of sleep they get. Sleeping well not only transforms your meditation practice, but can enhance your entire experience of life. It is absolutely the place to start.

Yet of course, it's inevitable that we will all have days when we're tired. Drowsiness is a valuable signal that we need more rest, but that doesn't mean we should go to sleep right this instant. Yet that is precisely the natural inclination when drowsiness arises during meditation. Drowsiness is a highly skilled manipulator, and it expertly lulls us deeper and deeper into its grasp. As we get pulled in, our senses dull and we lose awareness. That's the opposite of our goal in meditation.

Because drowsiness carries the valid message that you need more sleep, it's easy to buy into it and believe you should rest this very instant. Many of the obstacles to meditation are tricky in this way. They may have some basis, but that doesn't mean we should give into them. Even while recognizing that drowsiness is communicating an important message, we can still choose to not give into our sleepiness during meditation. Instead, we counteract it through a variety of remedies.

The most accessible and effective remedies for countering drowsiness involve changing our body's physiology. Caffeine takes this approach, but there are other methods that work well without any side effects. Our physiological arousal—and by extension our level of drowsiness—is immediately affected by whether our eyes are open or shut, the extent to which we engage our muscles, and the way we breathe. Each of these ways of changing our physiology provides a specific remedy to drowsiness, and we'll discuss each of them in turn.

Even though it makes it easier to get drowsy, most people prefer to meditate with their eyes closed. For one thing, closing your eyes can make it a little easier to focus on your anchor by removing potential visual distractions. But remember, you can't turn off peripheral awareness. Anyway, distractions are opportunities to practice the fundamental skills of attending and releasing. So as soon as drowsiness shows up, open your eyes. It's best to catch drowsiness as early as possible. You can also raise your gaze to eye level, allowing your gaze to just remain open without deliberately fixating on anything. These simple changes can make a big difference.

If you're quite drowsy, just opening your eyes won't be enough. The next step is to engage the muscles in your body a little more during meditation. Movement is a great source of energy, and it's possible to partially mimic that benefit by activating muscles even as you sit perfectly still. The most obvious and accessible way to do this is to just sit up a little taller. Engage the muscles in your belly and back so that you take a strong upright posture. You can also lift your hands and hold them—one on top of the other—near your belly button. I like to press one hand into the other with up to ten percent of my strength. This is so subtle that no one will know you're doing it, but it will activate the muscles in your upper back, shoulders, and arms. The goal isn't to engage your muscles as much as possible as if you were showing off your biceps, but to activate them just enough to hold you in a healthy alignment while generating energy.

Unless you're quite tired, opening your eyes and engaging more muscles in your body will usually do the trick. If it doesn't, another option is to change the way you're breathing. Rapid and forceful breathing stimulates the sympathetic nervous system, which you can think about as the gas pedal of your body. But even slow and deep breathing can help you stay alert if you can slow it down enough that is becomes just slightly challenging.

Opening your eyes, engaging your muscles, and changing your breathing are all good remedies to drowsiness. You should use them liberally when drowsiness shows up during your meditation. As a general rule, use any or all of these strategies as needed to stay alert during meditation. If you have applied them all and you're still drowsy, then try practicing while standing up or walking. Both of those options are far superior to passing the time in a quasi-slumber.

Each of the obstacles to meditation has not only specific remedies, but also an opposing quality. If an opposing quality is present in your mind, there will be less room for the obstacle. The opposing quality for drowsiness is enthusiasm.

I was chronically sleep deprived growing up. As a kid, I never managed to resolve the conflict between having to wake up early for school and believing that night was the most exciting time to be awake. This meant I was often tired and sometimes couldn't help but fall asleep in class. Yet with exactly the same amount of sleep, my energy would be through the roof when my alarm would go off at 6am on the days our school would take an end of the year trip to an amusement park. The difference, of course, was that I thought school was mostly boring but that the amusement park was exhilarating.

Enthusiasm can generate alertness even when we're not fully rested. This makes it a powerful tool for countering drowsiness. The trick is to make a habit of deliberately cultivating enthusiasm for mindfulness and meditation. Few people actively do this—and perhaps it even strikes you as an unusual thing to do—but it is highly effective. Mindfulness does after all hold the promise of improving your entire life and making you better able to make a meaningful difference in the lives of others. Connecting that incredible possibility to the simple act of sitting in meditation is a powerful strategy for countering drowsiness.

You can cultivate enthusiasm for mindfulness as a remedy to drowsiness when you feel tired, but you can also build your enthusiasm at other times. I like to start every meditation by reminding myself of some of the reasons why meditation is not only a worthwhile investment of time, but a genuinely exciting opportunity. As we'll discuss even more in later chapters, mindfulness is a crucially important skill in our pursuit of a reliable happiness. This means that meditation is a powerful tool for creating a fulfilling life. That's not something I want to sleep through.

25 - DISCOMFORT

Contemplative traditions don't always identify discomfort as a distinct obstacle to meditation, but I've found that it's one of the first and most frequent challenges that meditators face. Pain and discomfort are similar experiences that exist along a continuum of intensity. On one end, there is slight discomfort—like a room that is too warm or an itch on your nose. On the other end, when discomfort becomes more intense, we start calling it pain.

Although both pain and discomfort are inherently aversive, they're actually designed to protect us. They signal when something is wrong and motivate us to remedy the situation. Without discomfort, we wouldn't survive long. We know this because there are some individuals who are born with a rare genetic disorder that prevents them from being able to feel pain. What might seem like a blessing is actually a curse, and these individuals usually die early in life. One young boy who had this disorder died while trying to impress friends by jumping off the roof of a building. His decisions weren't calibrated by pain the way they should have been. When you or

I accidentally touch a hot stove, the immediate painful feedback is enough to make us careful in the future.

It often makes sense to listen and respond to discomfort, but discomfort is not always a reliable signal of what's best for you. Exercise is a good example. Even when you're working out safely with good form, it can still be quite uncomfortable. Within reason—and as long as you are not risking injury—it often makes sense to push on anyway.

This means that we need to distinguish between discomfort that is a genuine signal of risk versus discomfort that we can safely ignore. Strong and sharp pain usually signals risk, but there is no universal test to identify the discomfort we should obey. Fortunately, most people have strong intuitions based on their life experience, and you can develop greater discernment about discomfort over time by observing it carefully and noting its consequences.

Some discomfort is inevitable during meditation. We'll address the discomfort caused by sitting upright for extended periods of time before we discuss discomfort from other sources. Sitting upright with good posture can challenge our bodies in ways that can be quite uncomfortable. This is especially true for people living in sedentary cultures whose bodies have lost the strength and flexibility to sit comfortably in the upright postures most supportive of meditation. A great deal of the discomfort that arises during meditation is a consequence of an inflexible and unbalanced musculature.

The solution to this type of discomfort is to train your body to be able to sit comfortably during meditation. Over time, the act of sitting in meditation itself can improve your posture and mobility. I typically use the first several minutes of a meditation session to tune into my body and make several small shifts in my alignment so that I am ingraining healthy postural habits while meditating. Especially as you are cultivating a new posture, it's helpful to return your attention to your alignment periodically throughout the meditation as well. This becomes less and less necessary over time as good posture becomes your new default.

Although your posture and mobility can improve during meditation itself, the even more effective solution is to adjust the habitual ways you move and exercise throughout the rest of your life. If you have restrictions of mobility that make it hard to sit comfortably, you'll likely need to proactively address these restrictions by cultivating healthy movement patterns and using a few corrective exercises. Stretching right before meditation is also a great way to prepare your body to sit. You can find an overview of good meditation postures as well as mobility exercises that make sitting in meditation easier at this book's website at *http://empiricalwisdom.com/books*.

Developing a body that can sit comfortably will take a while. In the meantime, you'll need to know how to relate to the inevitable discomfort that will surface. Most importantly, if the discomfort you experience during meditation is severe or it feels like a warning signal of damage to your body, you should adjust your posture to address it. It's possible to strain your joints even while sitting still, and it would be counterproductive to sacrifice your physical health to practice mindfulness.

On the other hand, it's also counterproductive to adjust your posture every time you feel some discomfort. Acclimating to a new way of sitting will not always be comfortable, but small and temporary pains can often be ignored without any negative consequence. If you are not willing to experience a little bit of discomfort, you will spend too much time fixated on avoiding something that isn't a real problem. You'll be so busy tinkering with your posture that you'll never get a chance to settle in and further develop your meditation practice.

So what does this mean in practice? During the first few minutes of your meditation, make any needed adjustments to find a relatively comfortable posture where your body is in good alignment. Then once you've found a posture that feels right, commit to relative stillness unless you notice that you've slipped out of healthy alignment over time. Committing to physical stillness during meditation tends to echo into greater presence of mind. It also provides opportunities to notice and release urges to move that we normally indulge automatically. This helps our minds learn to concentrate even amidst discomfort, which is a crucial skill during both meditation and daily life. Yet there's no need to glorify stillness. If discomfort becomes your predominant experience—repeatedly capturing your attention despite your best efforts—simply make the needed adjustments to your posture in a deliberate way.

At some point, you will also experience discomfort during meditation that is not a direct result of sitting. Sometimes there will be nothing you can do to relieve this discomfort, so the task is to learn how to relate to it effectively. The typical reaction to discomfort is to immediately evaluate it as bad and to try to make it go away. This stops being a helpful response when there's no way to make the discomfort disappear. In that case, the negative evaluation of discomfort as a problem just serves to layer on more suffering. So as a first step, cultivate a willingness to just allow the discomfort to exist in your peripheral awareness. Occasionally it will pop into the spotlight of attention, at which point you can release it and refocus on your anchor. Even if this happens dozens or hundreds of times, remember that distraction is not a problem but an opportunity to practice releasing and attending.

However, pain can sometimes be so intense that we can barely help but focus on it. At this point, I like to make pain my anchor—not by focusing on the unpleasantness of it, but on the way that it shifts and transforms on almost a moment-by-moment basis. You can learn a lot about pain by watching it closely. It's possible to decenter from pain in a way that is similar to decentering from thoughts or emotions—recognizing that pain is transient and that our appraisal of pain as a problem can be subjective. You can step into the role of an observer, watching pain wax and wane without struggling over the struggle. The trick is to investigate the subtleties and transience of pain rather than to fixate on how bad it feels.

Discomfort is the only obstacle without a distinct opposing quality. Physical balance comes close because a body that is healthy and balanced is much less prone to discomfort. Yet even if you cultivate exceptional physical balance, you will still inevitably experience various pains and discomfort during meditation. Fortunately, the opposing quality to sensory desire—the sixth and final obstacle we'll discuss in this book—is also highly relevant to discomfort. Some of the strategies we'll introduce in that chapter will be directly applicable to discomfort as well. But before we go there, there are more pressing topics to cover first, starting with the obstacle of doubt. We'll tackle that one in the next chapter.

26 - DOUBT

Every obstacle is challenging in its own way, and doubt is uniquely effective at betraying us. It expertly convinces us of its value even as its undermines our progress. Keep in mind that the obstacles to meditation can convince us that they're not obstacles at all. They can do this because they often have an element of truth or value, at least in certain contexts. Drowsiness can be a genuine signal that you need more rest, yet we shouldn't be persuaded that meditation is the time to catch up on sleep. Pain often signals strain on your body, but it can sometimes be both healthy and necessary to sit through discomfort. Because it makes sense to listen to drowsiness and discomfort in some contexts, it takes discernment to avoid buying into them unnecessarily during meditation. Doubt—the next obstacle we'll discuss—presents us with a similar challenge but to an even greater extent.

Let's begin by examining why we need doubt in the first place. Doubt is crucial to a life well-lived because it helps us navigate a core human challenge: our minds are susceptible to believing things that aren't true. Relative to all other species, humans have a unique ability to use abstract concepts to understand and interact with the world. We can conceive of intangible things like democracy, the internet, or friends with benefits. Importantly, we can also use abstract concepts to understand things that are only true in some contexts (like the appropriateness of tapping a teammate's rear-end after a good play in a way that you would never do to a priest who just gave a great sermon). We can even use concepts to conceive of things that are only true hypothetically, like the fact that vampires can't tolerate sunlight.

Concepts are a powerful tool, but they are also responsible for a great deal of confusion and suffering. A key reason why this ability to use concepts carries such risk is that it also allows us to conceive of things that are untrue. We live in a world where the people around us sometimes communicate accurate information and sometimes share ideas that are simply false. This can happen through outright deception, but often it's just because the human mind is susceptible to believing in things that are untrue. For a long time, many people genuinely believed that the world was flat and witches were real. Some people still believe those things wholeheartedly. Other animals don't face this challenge the way we do. They don't have to sort out fake news from honest reporting. They don't live in a world where fact and fiction blend so frustratingly together.

In a world littered with pockets of confusion and deceit, doubt is our protector. It spares us from believing in advice or ideas that are harmful or untrue. Yet when doubt is misplaced, it can cause just as much trouble. It can stand in the way of our engaging with something of genuine benefit. There are two particularly common forms of doubt about meditation that make it hard to engage with this practice in the most effective way: doubt about the value of meditation and doubt about your own abilities. In both cases, it's important to address the underlying causes of your doubt so that you can cultivate the opposing quality of *confidence*: firm trust in the value of meditation and self-assurance in your ability to benefit.

Doubt about the value of meditation is actually the norm. Even though interest in mindfulness is growing quickly, most people still haven't had sufficient exposure to meditation to recognize it as a truly worthwhile pursuit. Even those who are interested in meditation typically still have some lingering doubts about it. Unless you are consistently practicing meditation on a daily basis, it's safe to say that you have some doubt about its value. It's not as simple as doubt either being present or absent—it exists along a continuum. So even if you believe meditation is valuable, you might not think it is as valuable as other ways you could spend your time.

If doubt in the value of meditation is not addressed, it can become a sort of self-fulfilling prophecy that prevents you from engaging with meditation in a productive way. The more we doubt meditation, the fewer opportunities we pursue to overcome that doubt.

Fortunately, confidence in the value of meditation is something you can cultivate proactively. In small ways, I reinforce my confidence in the value of meditation every day. This confidence can come from a variety of sources. First, understanding what mindfulness entails can go a long way because it's almost impossible to deny the value of being more able to skillfully guide your attention, thoughts, evaluations, and emotions toward the life you desire. Many people also gain confidence by looking to scientific research and learning that meditation not only improves people's lives but can also lead to measurable changes in the structure and function of the brain. Others gain confidence by spending time with people who have cultivated mindfulness to exceptional levels so that they can witness first-hand some of the benefits that come from meditating. All of these strategies are helpful, though the greatest confidence typically comes from a dedicated personal exploration of meditation under the guidance of some instruction that ensures you practice effectively. Often we need to experience the benefits of something ourselves before we can have full trust in it.

When doubt about the value of meditation arises while you're practicing, a helpful remedy is to recite a memorized phrase that can easily reconnect you with your personal and genuinely persuasive reasons for practicing. You might recall that when I want to generate enthusiasm for meditation, I reflect on the happiness it brings me. This is a two-for-one strategy because it also helps dispel any subtle doubt I might have about the value of meditation. So when doubt arises, I simply recite a short phrase—something like *meditation is the path to a truly reliable happiness*—once or twice to bring the benefits of meditation front and center in my mind. Then I return my attention to my anchor. What phrase could work for you?

The second common form of doubt concerns your personal capacity to excel at and benefit from meditation. This form of doubt often stems from believing that your personal capacity for mindfulness is limited—sometimes referred to as a fixed mindset. Like doubt about the value of meditation, this second kind of doubt also becomes a self-fulfilling prophecy. This happens through what we'll call belief-action-result cycles. Because you lack conviction in your capacity to improve at meditation (the belief), you don't practice consistently and wholeheartedly (the action), so you don't improve (the result).

This negative result then reinforces your original fixed mindset.

The remedy to doubt in your personal ability is proactively developing a growth mindset about your capacity for mindfulness. This means recognizing that your skill will inevitably improve with practice. There are two key ways to change a fixed mindset into a growth mindset. The first way is by targeting the belief itself, and you can do this by exposing yourself to new ideas and evidence that counter your limiting viewpoint. For instance, you could reflect on how countless people of all ages and backgrounds have benefitted from mindfulness training. You could also familiarize yourself with the considerable scientific evidence that meditation can help people with a wide range of initial abilities. These reflections can help you start to believe in your own ability, though cultivating a growth mindset also requires repeatedly choosing to endorse this belief. You can do this by simply releasing the fixed belief when it arises and directing your attention to a more empowering point of view. Eventually this process becomes automatic, and sooner or later the growth mindset will become your new default.

The second way to change a fixed mindset is by targeting the action instead. Typically, our beliefs dictate our actions, which dictate our results. But if you can find a way to change your actions even before your belief changes, you'll still start getting different results. Those results can give you the evidence you need to question your original fixed mindset. In the context of meditation, this might mean making a strong commitment to meditate every day for a month even if you're still unsure that you'll ever be able to improve. Although your lingering doubt will probably lower the quality of your practice, your willingness to meditate so consistently will still pay off over time—giving you some initial evidence of your capacity for improvement.

Of course, you can target the belief and the action simultaneously. When we offer mindfulness training as part of a research study, this is often the approach we take. We support people in questioning the merits of their fixed beliefs while also supporting them in taking massive action. After just a few weeks, the results they get are so dramatically different from what they're used to that their original fixed mindsets are simply no longer credible.

Doubt in your personal capacity to practice and benefit from meditation can show up with overwhelming force, like when someone concludes that their mind is so easily distracted that there's simply no hope for them. Alternatively, this kind of doubt can show up in more subtle ways. I often catch myself doubting my ability to go deeper in a given meditation when I have some major responsibility coming up that day that is capturing my attention. My doubt gives me a sort of permission to slack off, so I get caught by distracting thoughts more easily. When I notice this and deliberately foster some confidence in my ability, suddenly my meditation improves. You have to believe in your personal ability to go deeper. You turn the self-fulfilling prophecy on its head, letting your confidence rather than your doubt determine the quality of your meditation.

27 – ILL-WILL

You may be a very nice person, but I'm sure you still occasionally find yourself experiencing ill-will toward someone or something. Ill-will may sound like a strong word, but it exists along a continuum from mild negativity all the way to searing hatred. Most people only get to the point of hatred now and again, but a little negativity is a part of most of our daily lives. It's easy to feel little doses of ill-will toward both those we are closest to (that family member who always leaves dirty dishes in the sink) and also those we barely know at all (the stranger smacking gum in the movie theater). We can feel ill-will toward just about anything. Slow WIFI? Check. Stubborn belly fat? Check. Another long and challenging meditation? Check.

Ill-will is remarkably good at taking us out of the present moment. This is true no matter where our ill-will is directed, but it's particularly the case when we feel ill-will toward someone important in our life. I remember once spending almost an entire twenty-minute meditation ruminating about a challenging professional relationship while barely noticing my breath at all. Only when the timer rang at the end of the meditation did I snap out of rehashing my grievances and imagining hypothetical arguments. Ill-will was running the show, and I was along for the ride.

The ill-will we experience often feels justified, which makes it especially hard to let go. Let's face it, sometimes our ill-will is justified. Yet that doesn't necessarily mean that it's helpful. As the saying goes, harboring ill-will toward someone is like drinking poison and hoping they die. We are the ones who suffer most. Have you ever been upset with someone and they didn't even know it? You're carrying around the stress and burden of ill-will while they're just going about their day.

Sometimes the best solution to ill-will is to work things out with the person or to fix the situation. But it's also important to recognize that regardless of what happened, the experience of ill-will is ultimately generated by your reaction to the event. This means that, if you like, you can stop drinking poison. Mindfulness is not about running away from your problems, but it's crucial to recognize that many problems are sustained and exacerbated by how we think about them.

As with the other obstacles to meditation, you can often address ill-will by simply releasing it. Like other emotions, ill-will is fueled by our evaluations. If we choose to release those evaluations, our ill-will cannot sustain itself for long. Yet you may sometimes find that even though you keep trying to release your ill-will, you can't shake it off. When a more powerful strategy is needed, the opposing quality to ill-will is kindness. You can't feel sincere kindness toward someone and simultaneously stay mad at them. In fact, it's hard to genuinely feel kindness toward anything while harboring ill-will. In a given moment, the two experiences are mutually exclusive.

If you can foster kindness towards the source of your ill-will, that's great. When a neighbor is blasting music late at night, maybe you can still connect with the part of you that hopes they're having a good time. But that won't always be possible—sometimes it will feel too challenging. So the remedy to ill-will is to generate kindness *toward whatever you can*. It's easier to connect with a feeling of kindness toward someone you already feel positively about, so it often makes sense to start there. This might mean bringing to mind a close friend or family member and thinking about them in a way that generates a visceral experience of warmth and kindness. You might choose to think about what you appreciate about that person, why you are grateful for them, or how you wish them health and happiness. It doesn't have to be a person either—if puppies or kittens do the trick, great. Kindness toward yourself works too. After all, who wants to drink poison?

This approach of starting wherever is easiest is a common strategy used in meditations that are entirely devoted to generating kindness and compassion—sometimes called loving-kindness meditations. But you can also use this approach for just a short time as a way to counter the obstacle of ill-will during mindful breathing or present moment awareness. Once you've managed to connect to that feeling of warmth and kindness, you can try to extend that kindness to the source of your ill-will, but don't feel like you need to. You can often take the wind out of ill-will by simply generating a strong feeling of kindness toward anyone and then redirecting your attention back to your anchor.

One form of ill-will that you will likely experience at some point is ill-will toward meditation itself. Keep in mind, we don't always feel positively toward the things that are good for us. Few kids start out loving vegetables. Most adults never crave hard workouts. Sometimes the things that are best for us are challenging, and meditation can sometimes feel that way. When it's time to mediate on an ultra-busy day, it's easy to resent it. When your knee aches or your mind is growing impatient, it's easy to just want the meditation to be over. Ill-will toward meditation is a natural and common experience that you should anticipate experiencing at some point. This is especially true if you ever find yourself meditating according to someone else's schedule, which is usually the case at a meditation class or retreat. Ill-will toward meditation can show up in different ways, but it often manifests as frustration or resentment.

When you start to feel ill-will toward meditation, there's a specific remedy worth trying. I'll always remember how one of my earliest meditation teachers would describe meditation as a great friend. If you come across a best friend you haven't seen for a while, you feel happy just to be in their company. So when you notice ill-will toward meditation itself, try thinking about meditation as a true friend: someone who has your best interest at heart, who listens patiently to your scattered musings and grievances, and always leaves you a slightly better version of yourself. It might seem strange to personify meditation, but it can help to cultivate not only an appreciation of mindfulness but also a friendliness toward it. This approach may inspire a friendship that deepens for years to come.

28 - RESTLESSNESS

Let's face it, sitting quietly and watching the breath doesn't strike most people as riveting entertainment. While meditating, it's natural to find yourself wanting to do something else instead—if not by physically getting up, then at least by letting your mind wander. Yet this impulse to do something different is in direct opposition with the goal of being fully present right here.

Mental restlessness—the next obstacle—is hard to define because it can show up in many different ways. One signal that restlessness may be present during your meditation is a highly active mind. You might sit down to meditate but spend most of the time engaged in reflection, planning, or daydreaming. When we've asked participants in our studies to meditate on Friday afternoons, restlessness has often showed up for them as planning and excitement about the weekend. Restlessness can also show up as the feeling that you should be doing something else with your time. Alternatively, restlessness can manifest as a conscious feeling of dissatisfaction.

This last expression of restlessness is actually closest to

the ultimate source of this obstacle, which is feeling that something isn't right. If we want things to be different, it's hard to be present with things as they are. Often this feeling of dissatisfaction is so subtle that it goes unnoticed. In fact, it's relatively uncommon to find ourselves with literally no restlessness at all. In one way or another, we usually want things to be at least a little different than they are.

Depending on the source of your restlessness, it may be better to address it either on or off the cushion. Just as with the other obstacles, sometimes a solution needs to be proactively implemented outside of meditation. For instance, the best solution to drowsiness is consistent high-quality sleep, but meditation isn't the time to work off your sleep debt. If it's your lack of sleep at night that's the source of the problem, you need to resolve it outside of meditation. Similarly, given that unfinished work is often the source of restlessness, one effective strategy for countering restlessness is engaging more effectively with the various responsibilities of our lives. If we are behind on important tasks that require our attention, it's much more difficult to simply relax and be present. A legitimate feeling that something needs to get done pulls our mind out of the moment and into the responsibilities of daily life.

If unfinished work is the source of your restlessness, then one solution is to engage more appropriately with life's demands. We are *appropriately engaged* with an aspect of our lives when we have finished everything that we should have done by now. Of course, there will always be more to do in the future. It's possible to be appropriately engaged even though we still have a long to-do list. We just need to be on track. Being more appropriately engaged with something frees us from being inclined to think about that aspect of our lives in this moment, making it considerably easier to be mindful. Our minds are no longer distracted by nagging worries, missed deadlines, or unmet responsibilities.

The good news is that you are probably appropriately engaged with many aspects of your life already. For instance, maybe you have a backup key to your home so that you wouldn't have to change the locks if you lost your keys. Great, one less thing to have to worry about. Maybe you also have enough toothpaste and floss to last until at least the next time you're at the store. Kudos on your impressive foresight. Who knows…maybe you're even so on top of things that you've had your teeth professionally cleaned in the last six months, plus you have your next appointment on the books.

Or maybe you don't. It's a safe assumption that each of us could be more appropriately engaged with some part of our lives. Is there any little task around the house you've been putting off? Any emails in your inbox waiting for a response?

Achieving appropriate engagement in *every* aspect of our lives is an unrealistic standard for us mere mortals. You don't need to achieve that lofty ideal in order to start reaping the benefits of appropriate engagement. It's a continuum. The more appropriately engaged you are across the important dimensions of your life, the easier it will be for your mind to settle in and enjoy meditation.

Since it's unlikely that any of us will manage to get *all* our affairs in order, it's good to know that there are other strategies you can apply to counter restlessness. After all, it's inevitable that you will sometimes fall behind on things in life. And those unmet responsibilities will certainly try to interject themselves into your meditation, showing up again and again as stressful thoughts. This means that it's important to be able to let go of all our worldly responsibilities—even the ones that are past deadline—during the time of meditation. While you're practicing, give yourself permission to truly set everything else aside. The important things will still be waiting for you when you're done, and you'll have more of the presence of mind that you'll need to address them.

Regardless of the source of your restlessness, there's one particularly direct and potent remedy that you can apply when restlessness arises during meditation: cultivate appreciation of this moment. Restlessness is actually my favorite obstacle, only because I love this remedy. Bringing your attention to something positive about this moment is always possible. No matter how many things are out of place, a lot of things are also worthy of our gratitude. If you're still alive, many things must be going right. And besides the opportunity to live yet another day, what else could you appreciate right now? Maybe you're in a truly safe place. Maybe the temperature is comfortable. Maybe you're in the presence of people you enjoy. By cultivating appreciation for something about this moment, you generate a little more contentment with things as they are. It's no surprise then that the opposing quality of restlessness is contentment.

The more you are content with things as they are, the less restless you will feel. When you are content rather than bored in this moment, your mind has less incentive to rush off somewhere else. Why drift off into planning or fantasy when you're having a perfectly good time here and now? Occasionally you might even stumble into one of those moments where everything feels just right. In fact, if you are vigilant to restlessness and apply this remedy consistently, meditation will sometimes be a place where literally nothing feels out of place. Then your mind will be drawn into the moment rather than eager to change it.

29 – AN INTERLUDE ON RELIABLE HAPPINESS

You are so close to having all the strategies you need to excel at meditation, but there's still one huge obstacle to address. The last obstacle is sensory desire, and it can be a tough one. It's the most difficult obstacle to understand, which makes it one of the most challenging to overcome. To be able to understand and overcome sensory desire, it's extremely helpful to first take some time to reflect on the nature of happiness.

Humans seem to have a strong desire for lasting happiness and yet a poor track record of achieving it. Why the discrepancy? Perhaps we overestimate the actual priority of our desire for happiness. We may think that we are pursuing happiness when we go on a diet, hustle for a promotion, or get married—but is happiness the ultimate motivation behind these actions or does it just seem that way to us?

Our minds are a product of evolution, meaning they have been built with the fundamental goal to survive and reproduce. This orientation to survival and reproduction has been deeply ingrained in us by the slow and careful work of evolution. And yet this biological reality often feels unrepresentative of our subjective experience. After all, we have relatively little conscious interest in maximizing the number of our genes carried into future generations—something referred to as reproductive fitness. You may be strongly motivated to find a great partner, and perhaps you're even excited about the prospect of having kids or grandkids. Yet that's probably not because you care about how many copies of your serotonin transporter gene end up in the gene pool, right? How can we reconcile the fact that we don't consciously care about how many copies of our genes make it into future generations with the fact that it is our fundamental biological motivation?

Through a vast process of trial-and-error, evolution has discovered many ways of steering us toward reproductive fitness. Our minds are now filled with a constellation of specific motivations like thirst, hunger, and lust, as well as more abstract desires for things like belonging, status, and achievement. Throughout human evolution, the presence of each of these specific motivations has facilitated survival and reproduction, and so they have become deeply ingrained in our minds. We don't have to make a conscious decision to be hungry, find someone physically attractive, or care what others think about us. We do these things naturally just because we are human. In fact, doing these things was precisely what helped our ancestors survive and reproduce.

If many of our motivations are intrinsic to our evolutionary design rather than freely chosen, what compels us to pursue them? The answer to this question is simple and yet revealing because it helps explain why happiness seems like our driving motivation even when it's not. We're compelled by our motivations because they are linked to either pleasure or pain. Hunger is painful, and increasingly so until it is satiated. Sex is pleasurable, particularly until the deed is done. Pleasure is the carrot enticing us forward and pain is the stick if we don't comply. Moral philosopher Jeremy Bentham went as far as to argue that "pain and pleasure govern us in all we do, in all we say, and in all we think."

Because we're constantly taking action to pursue pleasure and avoid pain, happiness can seem like our fundamental motivation. Yet happiness serves as an incentive to take action rather than the underlying biological objective. The biological objective is not to be happy. It's to survive and reproduce. In order to motivate us to do that, our evolutionary design occasionally allows us to feel happy when we're making progress toward that more fundamental goal. This can be difficult to grasp and accept, but I've found that understanding it is crucial to having a genuine chance at creating a reliable happiness in our lives.

Even when we feel that we are directly striving for happiness, the unconscious goal that is ultimately motivating our actions is often reproductive fitness. We don't realize that happiness is only the rewarding byproduct. This is illustrated by many people's unwillingness to accept hypothetical deals in which they are offered true happiness but must sacrifice the things they usually associate with happiness. For example, people often reject true happiness if it were to require social isolation or unattractiveness, even just after saying that they strive for connection and beauty in order to be happy. This highlights the human tendency to overlook the real source of our motivations. We might think that we want to be attractive in order to be happy, but if that were our real motivation we should gladly trade beauty for happiness.

So the common notion that we are fundamentally oriented toward happiness turns out to be only a half-truth. We do have a hard-wired preference for pleasure over pain, and how we feel is an extremely powerful motivator. This makes it tempting to conclude that maximizing our joy while minimizing our suffering is our fundamental aim. This may even be our conscious wish, but it is probably not the ultimate goal behind the majority of our actions. Instead, the powerful motivations that assist our survival and reproduction are running the show, and they use pain and pleasure as leverage.

If pain and pleasure motivate us to do things that will ultimately increase our reproductive fitness, then anything more enduring than flickering happiness may be disadvantageous from the perspective of evolution. If one good meal removed the experience of hunger for a year, that would be a serious design flaw. From the perspective of evolution, enduring satisfaction is a problem. We have to be dissatisfied for the promise of future satisfaction to motivate us. Enduring satisfaction could make us less likely to invest time and energy in maximizing our attractiveness, building our influence, or jostling for the best possible mate. Happiness is a useful motivator precisely because it doesn't last. This is the basis of the metaphorical *hedonic treadmill* on which we all run—chasing happiness, enjoying it only briefly with each new success, and then chasing again. We run after happiness our entire lives and never seem to be able to hold on to it.

Your happiness is not evolution's top priority. Unfortunately, this means we are simply not designed for lasting happiness. This is the reality of our situation, but that doesn't mean we need to resign to a life of discontent. By recognizing the limitations of our evolutionary design, we open the possibility of moving beyond it. Evolution has done a breathtakingly good job at preparing us to meet its objectives of survival and reproduction, but cultivating a reliable happiness is up to us.

So how do most people try to increase their happiness? One common approach is trying to fill your life with more sensory pleasures. Many people try to expertly string together good music, tasty food, beautiful views, and novel entertainment. The challenge, of course, is that these things are not always available. Even when they are, the satisfaction they provide is inherently short-lasting. It's impossible to have a life of endless sensory pleasures, and when the pleasures drop away so does the happiness.

Another common approach for trying to increase happiness is to accumulate good circumstances. It's easy to believe that we would be happy if we could just get the right job, spouse, friends, body composition, bank account, car, or house. Of course, accumulating and maintaining all these things is no simple task. Many people strive their entire lives to get things just right and never succeed. And even if we manage to get impressively close, we tend to get used to good circumstances. The longer we have them, the harder it is to truly appreciate them. Many people find a lot of enjoyment in getting a new car, but the excitement fades as the car becomes just another routine detail of their lives.

Both of these approaches—accumulating sensory pleasures and good circumstances—can provide some additional happiness. They are both worth pursuing as long as they don't distract you from an alternate approach that would actually be more effective in the long run.

What is that approach? If you want a truly reliable happiness, then the source of that happiness can't be from anything external. As Austrian psychiatrist and Holocaust survivor Viktor Frankl famously said, "When we are no longer able to change a situation, we are challenged to change ourselves." Given that you have quite limited control over the world around you, the only viable approach is to cultivate the conditions for enduring happiness in your own mind. This is something no one can take away from you.

Cultivating reliable happiness may sound far-fetched, but by now you actually have most of the strategies you will need. The most important skills to cultivate are ones we've already mentioned: the ability to direct your thoughts, make skillful evaluations, manage your emotions, and find gratitude in all the things you do have. And because mindfulness makes all these things possible, it is the master skill. It is the path to a truly reliable happiness. Yet there is still one last obstacle to meditation—sensory desire—that you will need to overcome. Now that you're prepared with some perspective on happiness, you're ready to face sensory desire head on.

30 – SENSORY DESIRE

Our research team has spent several years investigating the impact of mindfulness training in high schools, and we usually introduce meditation to youth with mindful eating. Students walk into the first class to find a clementine sitting on their meditation cushion. What would normally take just a minute to eat, we stretch into a five minute exploration of sensation. We guide students to bring their attention to every taste, smell, and sound of peeling and eating the fruit. When the exercise is complete and we ask for reflections, at least one student always shares that it was the best clementine they had ever tasted. This can be a dramatic insight for students, ushering in a new appreciation of how they can control their attention to change their experience.

This mindful eating exercise serves to pique students' interest while introducing them to the practice of meditation, but it regrettably also sets up an implicit expectation that mindfulness is about enhancing sensory experiences. By bringing our minds fully into the present moment, our sensations can become more intense. We're no longer distracted from them. So mindfulness can enhance sensory pleasures, and this can be a source of motivation to practice. Nevertheless, sensory desire—craving certain kinds of sensory experiences—is one of the most potent obstacles to meditation. Sensory desire can refer to both the things we want to experience (like great music) as well as those we want to avoid (like loud traffic).

It's not that there's anything wrong with sensory pleasures. Nothing could be more natural than to enjoy things like great food, music, weather, and entertainment. Sometimes pursuing these pleasures is genuinely good for us, like when we prepare a healthy and delicious meal. It's also true that we do often derive at least a momentary happiness from sensory pleasures. So why are they an obstacle to meditation?

To appreciate the challenge of sensory desire, it's helpful to start by considering its opportunity cost—a phrase from economics that refers to what else you could get for the same investment of time and money. For the price of an extravagant dinner out, you might be able to have five meals prepared at home. The opportunity cost of two more hours at work to finish an important project is two hours you could be spending with your family. So what is the opportunity cost of pursuing sensory desires?

The greatest risk of sensory desire is that the constant pursuit of temporary pleasures can distract us from cultivating more enduring sources of happiness. So the opportunity cost of sensory desire is the time we could invest more wisely. Every person I know—myself included—has fallen prey to this risk. Our modern world is filled with endless temptations. For those of us who have spent more time in our lives watching television than cultivating our minds through meditation, there's a reasonably good chance that sensory desire has distracted us from more reliable sources of happiness.

We are hard-wired to value sensory pleasures, so we spend a lot of time thinking about and pursuing them. Yet sensory pleasures are inherently transient, so they offer us only passing contentment. A piece of your favorite cake may bring you pleasure while you eat it, but that joy doesn't last. No amount of mindfulness can change that. This means that if we want enduring contentment, we must eventually accept that we will not find it in even the most attractive combinations of sights, sounds, scents, and flavors.

Many people go through their lives believing that they need their sensory desires to be satisfied in order to be happy, but this belief puts your happiness at the mercy of your circumstances. If you ever achieve a reliable happiness, it won't be because of the things that are happening to you. It will come from cultivating your mind—especially your ability to direct your attention toward skillful thoughts, evaluations, and emotions. This recognition can actually bring a sense of relief, because it frees us from trying to do the impossible: making the world conform to our desires so that we can finally be happy. You can spend your entire life struggling endlessly to pave the world in leather or you can wise up and invest in a good pair of sandals.

The recognition that sensory pleasures will never provide the happiness we desire allows for an empowering shift of priorities. We become free to dedicate a little more of our time and attention to the more reliable causes of happiness, including meditation. We can still make plenty of time to enjoy the countless pleasures of life, but we can also pursue something even more worthwhile. It's a process of transcending the familiar in order to pursue something greater. In this case, that means transcending the impulse to constantly chase sensory pleasures so that we can dedicate a little more time to meditation. Transcendence is the opposing quality to sensory desire. I know that's a lofty word, but it's fitting because this is a fairly elevated way to experience your life.

So far we've described sensory desire as an obstacle to meditation because it leads you to misallocate your time—we chase sensory pleasures for hours while struggling to find even thirty minutes to meditate. In simply choosing to meditate rather than seek pleasure elsewhere, we are letting go of a great deal of sensory desire. But sensory desire can also be an obstacle while we meditate. In fact, one way to think about meditation is as a gradual process of releasing sensory desire little by little.

Most people start meditating with a natural hope that it will provide them with pleasurable experiences. We want the clementine to taste especially sweet. We hope meditation will produce a pleasant tranquility. Yet while pleasure can certainly arise during meditation, it shouldn't be the goal. The goal is to hone the skills of attending and releasing, as well as your ability to apply those skills to influence your state of mind. If meditation becomes just another realm where we chase sensory pleasures, we will inevitably become frustrated when it doesn't produce them.

Just as importantly, getting swept up in sensory desire will also make it harder to progress in your practice. Sensory desire during meditation generally makes it more difficult to stay with your anchor. A good example is physical discomfort and the natural impulse to want to be free of it. As we've discussed, some discomfort is inevitable during meditation. Yet a strong desire to be free from discomfort makes it hard to be okay with an ache in your back or the room being too hot. Sensory desire leads these kinds of discomforts to capture our attention much more than they need to.

When we release sensory desires, it becomes easier to let our minds settle on our anchor. Of course, that's easier said than done. If simply trying to release sensory desire isn't enough to loosen its grip on your mind during meditation, the remedy is to recall the shortcomings of sensory pleasures. This first requires getting very clear on what those shortcomings are through reading, reflection, and observation of your own experience. Then it's much easier to quickly bring that understanding to mind during meditation. When you can see the object of your desire for what it is—recognizing that it will at best provide you with only a temporary satisfaction—it becomes easier to truly let it go.

Even after we learn to let go of most of our sensory desires during meditation, it's often still hard to disengage from the mundane sensory experiences that distract us from our anchor. Although it's not typically how we think of the word desire, most of us have a strong inclination to pay attention to our sensory experiences. Even if we're not desiring any particular experience, we can still have a subtle desire to keep experiencing sensations. This more subtle impulse to stay involved in our sensory experiences is another aspect of sensory desire, broadly construed. This is part of the reason why sensory deprivation can be a form of torture for the untrained mind. We crave sensory experiences, and we spend almost our entire lives enveloped in them. The more attached we are to our sensory experiences, the harder it is to release them so that we can fully direct our attention elsewhere. So during meditation, we continue the process of letting go of sensory desire by releasing even this more subtle attachment to sustaining awareness of something besides our anchor. During mindful breathing, for example, we release our inclination to engage with our senses of sight, touch, sound, and smell in order to focus on just the sensations of the breath.

Progressing in meditation involves letting go of sensory desire little by little, but that doesn't translate into experiencing less and less pleasure. In fact, the more you release sensory desire, the deeper and more pleasant meditation becomes. To an extent, the same pattern can be true in daily life. When I go awhile without listening to music, I find even more enjoyment in the songs I do hear. And when I'm not chasing sensory pleasures, I sometimes stumble into them in unexpected ways without even trying—noticing and enjoying little things around me that I would have otherwise missed altogether. But of course, the point of deprioritizing sensory desire isn't to get more sensory pleasure. It's to gain something even more valuable: a mind that is capable of finding happiness regardless of circumstances. Each time you release a little more sensory desire, you create the opportunity to experience a little more reliable happiness. That happiness will provide the encouragement you need to go further.

Part V:

MASTERY

31 – ESTABLISHING THE HABIT OF MEDITATION

Watching football every Sunday doesn't turn you into an NFL quarterback. Simply reading diet books and designing hypothetical workout programs doesn't get you in shape. Similarly, you can't expect that reading a book on meditation— or even a dozen books—will make you an expert. Reading can only empower you to practice well. The real gains happen from actually practicing.

Many people who take an interest in meditation find it challenging to develop a consistent daily practice. Even when we know something is good for us, we may still struggle to do it. Just think of all the New Year's resolutions that don't last past January. Let's face it: we often have good intentions but only mediocre follow through. The gap between what you know you should do and what you actually do is often the distance between the life you want and the life you have.

One way to increase our consistency in meditation is to deliberately establish a habit of daily practice. We all have hundreds of deeply ingrained habits that we already do each day. Odds are, you flush the toilet after you use it. Once upon a time, you had to learn this behavior, but now it has become so ingrained that you do it automatically. Thankfully, most everyone else does too.

Some of our habits are beneficial while others are quite harmful. Either way, it's the cumulative nature of habits that makes them powerful. They can uplift or destroy us little by little. One cigarette won't kill you, but smoking every day easily could. One meditation won't provide you with great skill in attending and releasing, but daily meditation will.

So how do we create a new habit? It's much easier if we decide on three things in advance: what we'll do, when we'll do it, and how we'll enjoy the process.

First, consider how long you want to meditate each day. It's important to choose a goal that's realistic for you. If you're new to meditation, consider starting with a commitment to sit at least five minutes a day. If at the end of those five minutes you feel like sitting longer, go for it. This is a useful approach because it's much harder to come up with good excuses to skip meditation when your commitment is just five minutes. Everyone can find five minutes a day. If you set too lofty a goal, you will either make excuses to skip or you will end up feeling resistance or ill-will toward meditation. This can be avoided by starting small and gradually increasing the duration of your practice. Over time, you can work up to half an hour or longer each day. If you decided to start a jogging routine for the first time, you wouldn't start by trying to jog six miles a day. You would start small and build up to longer distances. You can apply this same logic to your meditation practice.

Once you know how long you plan to meditate, you need to decide when you're going to practice each day. This is a crucially important step. Habits are easiest to establish if you can always meditate at the same time of day and at the same location, but that may not be feasible for you seven days a week. For instance, you may have to choose different times for weekdays and weekends. The important thing is to decide in advance. If you can, try to choose a time and place when something about your environment will help you remember to practice. For example, maybe you'll meditate right after you brush your teeth in the morning regardless of what time you wake up. Over time, brushing your teeth will then actually help remind you to meditate. Whatever you decide, put it on your calendar. Set a reminder. Tell your partner. Make it official. Of course, if over time you recognize that you chose a less than ideal time, you can always change it.

Finally, the third step is accentuating the enjoyment we experience during and immediately after meditation. It's much easier to establish the habit of doing something rewarding than doing something we dread. You can find deliberate ways to enhance the experience of meditation. For instance, you might choose to start your meditation by reminding yourself how nice it is to have some time to set down all of your burdens and deeply relax. When you finish meditating, you might choose to savor how good it feels to have practiced, to notice how it affects your body and mind, and to congratulate yourself for doing something that's good for so many areas of your life. Taking a moment to let these things sink in will make establishing the habit of meditation much easier.

By clarifying these three things in advance, you'll be able to establish the habit of daily meditation much more easily. So…how long do you plan to practice? When are you going to do it? And how will you accentuate your enjoyment of the process?

In addition to creating a daily meditation habit, I'd also

recommend using the same approach to support your practice of mindfulness during daily life. The ambitious intention to practice mindfulness all day long is great, but it can also be strategic to pick just a few times each day that you truly commit to being mindful. Consider starting by picking times in your day when you tend to mind-wander through something that has the potential to be quite enjoyable. Washing your hands, hugging another person, or eating dinner can all become strong cues for mindfulness. These dedicated pockets of mindfulness can eventually become truly habitual, occurring automatically even without your deliberate intention. These moments can also provide a great platform for extending mindfulness into the rest of your daily life. Much like how a positive morning routine can translate into an all-around better day, choosing small activities during which you will be habitually mindful can inspire continued presence of mind throughout the day.

For most people, developing a strong habit of meditation doesn't happen spontaneously. Ensuring that it happens takes a little strategic planning, but it's well worth the effort. Among all the things that we know we should do each day, meditation can become one of the most enjoyable and rewarding. It's worth putting in the effort to cultivate a daily meditation practice, at least until it's developed into a strong habit. Then it will cultivate you.

32 – MASTERY OF MINDFULNESS

At this point, you know how to use mindfulness to dramatically improve your life. The question now becomes: will you do it?

Most people have superficial relationships with the most important things in life. Many of us struggle to maintain high levels of health and fitness. The majority of marriages dissolve, and only a small fraction of couples manage to sustain a deep love and connection over the long term. And strikingly few people ever develop true mastery of their minds—their attention, thoughts, evaluations, and emotions. Mastery of the most important things in life is tragically rare.

One reason so few of us develop mastery in these areas is simply because we're not taught how to do so—or at least not taught well. I sat through four years of high school classes without being explicitly taught a single thing about how to navigate intimate relationships or even how to navigate my emotions. Of course, many of us who are teachers and parents struggle in these areas ourselves, making it difficult to instill mastery in the next generation. Yet these days anyone truly committed to developing mastery of their mind, body, or relationships can find the guidance they need. For every dimension of our lives, there are 1000 apps, books, and coaches who can help.

A less obvious but major obstacle to developing mastery is that we learn throughout our lives that superficial engagement can often be beneficial. Many things in life have diminishing marginal returns, meaning that for every additional amount of effort you make, the additional reward is a little less than the one before. Brushing your teeth is a good example. If you go from not brushing your teeth at all to brushing one minute a day, the rewards are tremendous. The second minute also brings substantial benefit. The third and fourth are still helpful, but less so. After say six minutes a day, there's likely almost no benefit.

Because so many things in life have diminishing marginal returns, many of us learn to do just enough. We try to do the least possible that's necessary to get the grade we want, to get in good shape, or to keep our partner happy. Over time and for good reason, this becomes our predominant strategy. We adopt a do-just-enough mindset. When it comes to brushing our teeth, it's the right strategy. Yet there are also things in life with increasing marginal returns—meaning that as you invest more, the benefits you receive become even greater. In these cases, the do-just-enough mindset falls short.

I first remember learning this lesson at basketball camp when I was twelve. The camp was hosted by the Philadelphia 76er's and included some instruction from professional NBA players. One day a player taught us the optimal form for shooting a basketball and how we should practice by standing close to the basket and drilling in the right form over and over. Then we had some time to just practice on our own. After only a few minutes of trying his strategy, I watched as dozens of middle school and high school kids got bored and instead started shooting 3-point shots, half court shots, or even shots from out of bounds over the backboard. Meanwhile the guy who was already getting paid a million dollars a year to play the game he loved was off in the corner of the room standing just five feet away from the basket and practicing over and over exactly what he had taught us. He knew that developing mastery of the fundamentals was key to success. As I watched him, I recognized that true mastery of the right things can lead to dramatic rewards.

Several years later, I learned this lesson in a different way from my dad. I was in college and feeling uneasy because I couldn't decide whether to pursue a career in academia, environmental advocacy, or business. He could tell that I mistakenly thought everything was riding on making the right choice. He told me that because all the options I was considering were worthwhile, the more important thing was developing true mastery in whatever I chose. Society tends to reward true excellence. If you strive for your personal best and create as much value for others as possible, that investment eventually starts to pay increasing marginal returns. It might not come in the first year or even the first decade, but eventually your professional mastery makes it possible for you to make wiser and grander contributions. So my dad's advice was that I was right to carefully weigh all my options, but that I should also trust that with a commitment to mastery any path I chose would be a rewarding adventure.

Your career isn't the only part of life where striving for mastery can produce increasing marginal returns. Mindfulness works this way too. If you dabble in mindfulness, you will get some benefit but not that much. You wouldn't expect that going for a jog once a month would keep you in shape, right? If you practice regularly by finding opportunities to bring mindfulness into daily life and spending at least a few minutes every day in formal practice, then you will likely benefit a lot over time. And if you go even further and make a commitment to develop mastery in mindfulness, it can change everything. As we've discussed, the way we direct our attention shapes our entire experience of life. The fundamental skills of mindfulness—attending and releasing—are some of the most important skills you can develop because you can use them to influence your thoughts, evaluations, and emotions.

Mastery of mindfulness isn't about being better than others. Unlike professional basketball, it's not about belonging to an elite class of professionals a tier above the rest. It's about having true command over your attention so that you can choose to skillfully guide your mind from moment to moment. This kind of mastery is available to anyone who is willing to put in the work.

When I think about my daughter, the thing I most hope that she will master is mindfulness. Of course I want her to develop mastery in her health, relationships, and career, but I know how much mastery of mindfulness will accelerate her progress in these other areas. Mastery of mindfulness makes all our other efforts at personal development more efficient because we actually have influence over our minds. If we decide we want to get in better shape, we don't have to fight against a rebellious mind the entire way. If we decide we want to cultivate gratitude, we can direct our mind toward appreciation a hundred times a day rather than maybe ten.

This ability to skillfully direct our minds is a key reason why mindfulness has increasing marginal returns. The better you get at it, the more you will benefit. Let's imagine that you now spend about ten percent of your waking life with your mind directed to the right thing, at the right time, and in the right way. Now imagine that through a commitment to cultivating mindfulness, you manage to increase that rate to twenty percent. A ten percent increase isn't an outrageous goal. You could do that—having made it through this entire book, you now have the necessary perspective and strategies. On a typical day, you would then be skillfully directing your mind for three hours rather than one and a half. That's probably enough to make the difference between having a good or bad day, but an extra 90 minutes of time well spent isn't going to change your entire life. Yet if you extend that difference out every day over a typical adult lifespan, you would spend over 30,000 more hours making moments count.

There's a widespread idea that has emerged over the last decade that it takes 10,000 hours to become a true expert in something. Although this popular belief is not exactly true, it can still provide some useful context. Whatever you do consistently is who you become. How different would your mental habits be if 30,000 more hours of your life were spent in a way that cultivated your presence, gratitude, and connection to others?

If you think you could aspire to even more than a ten percent increase in your mindfulness, what if we took it further? Keep in mind that mindfulness can become self-accelerating. If you can take your level of mindfulness from ten to twenty percent of the day, you will naturally start drifting toward thirty. If you truly commit to mastery and manage to spend fifty percent of your waking life directing your attention skillfully, then you would spend an extra 126,000 hours with your mind in a good place. That's 7,884 days. Twenty two years. How different might your life be then?

The moments of our life pass by and don't come back. Reflecting on the two years since my daughter was born, I'm grateful for all the times that my commitment to mastering mindfulness helped me be truly present with her. I'm grateful for all the times our eyes locked. For all the times I watched her fill with pride and glee as she did something she had never done before. For all the silly faces and grins and cuddles. It's moments like these that make presence of mind indispensable to me. If I'm lucky enough to have another twenty two years of moments with her, I'd like to be fully present for as many of them as possible.

AFTERWORD

Mindfulness offers enormous benefits, but it provides it in tiny doses. Each moment becomes an opportunity to cultivate your state of mind. Just remember, *this* is the moment when it happens. If you're willing to wait for the next, you'll wait forever.

ABOUT THE AUTHORS

Michael Mrazek, Ph.D. is the director of research at the University of California's Center for Mindfulness & Human Potential. His research identifies innovative ways to increase the effectiveness of mindfulness training, particularly in high schools. He also tests the limits of how much a person can improve through intensive evidence-based training programs that target health, mindfulness, and self-control. Michael designs and teaches research-based mindfulness retreats, as well as an academic course on the science and practice of mindfulness. He also serves as the CEO of Empirical Wisdom, an online training and coaching firm.

Alissa Mrazek, Ph.D. is a post-doctoral research fellow at the University of California's Center for Mindfulness & Human Potential. Her research focuses on refining evidence-based strategies for enhancing self-control and mindfulness, with an emphasis on how these two skills are mutually reinforcing. She also serves as Chief Scientific Officer of Empirical Wisdom.

Kaita Mrazek is a visiting researcher at the University of California Santa Barbara, Chief Marketing Officer of Empirical Wisdom, and director of the ambassador program for Ghost Flower Activewear. Kaita received degrees in Dance and Psychology before discovering Yoga and Pilates as vehicles for her continued exploration of the relationship between body and mind. Her work integrates the best of many physical disciplines into an optimal approach to enhancing health and fitness.

Made in the USA
Lexington, KY
05 October 2017